008367

KT-166-099

Practical
TREE MANAGEMENT

AN ARBORISTS HANDBOOK

Trevor Lawrence,
Paul Norquay
and Karl Liffman

Figure 1 An excellent specimen of Yellow Box (*Eucalyptus melliodora*) growing naturally.

Inkata Press
MELBOURNE • SYDNEY

INKATA PRESS
A DIVISION OF BUTTERWORTH-HEINEMANN

AUSTRALIA   BUTTERWORTH-HEINEMANN 271–273 Lane Cove Road, North
                   Ryde 2113
                   BUTTERWORTH-HEINEMANN 18 Salmon Street, Port Melbourne
                   3207

UNITED KINGDOM   BUTTERWORTH-HEINEMANN Oxford

USA   BUTTERWORTH-HEINEMANN Stoneham

National Library of Australia Cataloguing-in-Publication entry

---

Lawrence, Trevor, 1951– .
  Practical tree management.

  Bibliography.
  Includes index.
  ISBN 0 909605 72 6.

  1. Trees, Care of — Handbooks, manuals, etc. 2. Aboriculture —
  Handbooks, manuals, etc. I. Norquay, Paul, 1950– . II. Liffman,
  Karl, 1954– . III. Title.

635.977

© 1993 T. Lawrence, P. Norquay and K. Liffman
Published by Reed International Books Australia Pty Limited trading as Inkata Press

This book is copyright. Except as permitted under the Copyright Act 1968 (Cth), no part of this
publication may be reproduced by any process, electronic or otherwise, without the specific
written permission of the copyright owner. Neither may information be stored electronically in
any form whatsoever without such permission.

Enquiries should be addressed to the publisher.

Designed by John van Loon
Typeset in 9½ pt Palatino by Bookset Pty Ltd
Printed in Australia by Impact Printing, Melbourne

WARWICKSHIRE COLLEGE
LIBRARY

Class No:
  635.977

Acc No:
  00503615

635.977

008367

94

96

Practical
TREE MANAGEMENT
AN ARBORISTS HANDBOOK

WITHDRAWN

LIBRARY

WARWICKSHIRE
COLLEGE

Warwickshire College

* 0 0 5 0 3 6 1 5 *

Contents

Acknowledgements

Initial typing of the manuscript was carried out by Lynda Hynd. Final wordprocessing of the manuscript was undertaken by Heather Sims. This work was not easy as it entailed making numerous alterations.

Photographs in this publication were taken by Rob Ball, David Bennett, Hiliary Griffith, Patricia Liffman and the authors. The *Bendigo Advertiser* provided the photograph of the lopped plane trees at Huntly, Victoria in the 'Pruning' chapter. Stihl Pty Ltd assisted in the provision of artwork for the chapter 'Chainsaw Servicing and Safety'.

The excellent illustrations in this book are the work of Chris Preston. Sketches of insects were ably completed by Julia McLeish.

Specifications for steel wire rope in the 'Bracing' chapter were largely obtained from Australian Wire Industries.

In the chapter 'Tree growth and development', the tree trunk cross sections are reproduced from J.S. Yeates and Ella O. Campbell *Agricultural Botany* (Government Printing Office, New Zealand) and the diagram representing buds with a protective covering of scale leaves is reproduced from David Kilpatrick *Pruning for the Australian Gardener*. Exploded views of branch and trunk collars have been taken from A.L. Shigo *A New Tree Biology* (Shigo and Trees Associations, USA). The diagram representing compartmentalisation has been adapted from that on page 13 of A.L. Shigo *Tree Decay: An Expanded Concept* (US Department of Agriculture). The plant nutrient diagram in the 'Maintaining tree health' chapter is reproduced from *Soils: An outline of their properties and management* (CSIRO Division of Soils).

The City of Bendigo, City of Ballaarat, Royal Botanic Gardens, Melbourne, and Steven Hains, Arborist, Beaufort have also assisted in the provision of artwork.

Dr Peter Yau, Arboriculturalist, City of Melbourne; John Hawker, Horticulturalist, Urban Design Unit, Department of Planning and Environment, Melbourne; Dr Dan Neely, Editor, *Journal of Arboriculture*, Illinois, USA; Brian Simpson, Arborist, Melbourne; David Grant, Arborist, City of Ballaarat; and Max Jeffery, Proprietor, Jefferys Chainsaw Service, Harcourt, Victoria, have all provided assistance greatly appreciated by the authors.

About the book

This publication is a practical handbook on an aspect of arboriculture known as tree surgery. Some of the topics discussed in this text include: climbing, pruning, bracing, wound and cavity treatments, branch and tree removal and chainsaw maintenance.

The inspiration for compiling this book came from the need to provide practical and relevant reference notes for students of horticulture.

The authors

Trevor Lawrence (City and Guilds of London Cert. Tree Surgery) is a self-employed tree surgeon from Ballarat, Victoria. Previously, Trevor worked as a tree surgeon in the Royal Parks Department in London and also in local government parks and gardens departments in metropolitan Melbourne, Victoria. He has served on Advisory Committees responsible for the development and implementation of post-apprenticeship courses in arboriculture in Victoria and is employed as a sessional tree surgery instructor by the Victorian College of Agriculture and Horticulture, Burnley, Loddon Campaspe College of TAFE, Bendigo, and School of Mines, Ballarat, Victoria.

Paul Norquay (Dip.Hort., TTIC) is employed as a teacher of trade gardening students in Ballarat, Victoria. Before working at Ballarat, Paul spent a number of years at the Victorian College of Agriculture and Horticulture, Burnley, where he was the College's first lecturer in arboriculture. A great deal of his time was spent teaching the practical aspects of tree surgery from the time when arboriculture and tree surgery were first recognised as specialist disciplines in Australia. While working at VCAH, Burnley, Paul was also involved in the development and implementation of tertiary courses in arboriculture at the College. He has also worked for local government parks and gardens departments and in commercial arboriculture.

Karl Liffman (B.Ed., Dip.Hort.Sci.) is a self-employed horticulturalist and part-time teacher of trade gardening students, from Maldon, Victoria. He has worked in plant nurseries, for local government parks and gardens departments, and as a full-time TAFE horticultural trades teacher in Victoria. Karl has also been involved in the development of TAFE courses in horticulture and turf management.

Warning and disclaimer

Every effort has been made to ensure that the techniques described in this publication comply with currently accepted industry standards. However, many techniques are potentially hazardous, especially for those who are inexperienced or poorly supervised.

Reference to any product or type of equipment does not necessarily imply endorsement. Before using any product, check that it complies with statutory standards. Read and follow cautions and directions with the utmost care.

Neither the authors nor the publishers take any responsibility for the precision of information contained herein.

Introduction

This book is primarily concerned with tree surgery which is the aspect of arboriculture dealing with tree maintenance. Arboriculture is a branch of horticulture. As well as tree surgery, arboriculture includes the production, selection, planting, cultivation and maintenance of woody plants (mainly trees) for the benefit, both practical and aesthetic, of the community.

There are many publications available on these specialised areas of arboriculture but it is hoped that this text will provide up-to-date information on practical techniques which may not be available from other sources.

As the treatment of the subject matter presented is fairly broad, other references may need to be consulted for a detailed study of specific topics. These are listed under 'References and further reading'.

As many of the operations described in this text are potentially dangerous, strict adherence to proper safety precautions is of paramount importance.

Figure 2   A Manna Gum (*Eucalyptus viminalis*) of habitat value.

The value of trees

Trees are a very precious resource; their value in the environment is far-reaching and should not be underestimated.

Among the many valuable functions performed by trees are air purification, soil stabilisation, provision of shade and protection from wind. In addition, many trees are important for their production of timber, fruit and other commodities. The presence of trees may influence weather patterns as well as improving the aesthetics of the landscape. It can take many years for a tree to grow to its full stature and potential and, in so doing, it may also provide a significant historical link with the past.

Figure 3   An Indian Bean Tree (*Catalpa bignonioides*) of amenity value.

In an urban situation it is desirable, for the good of the community, that trees be maintained for as long as possible in a healthy, safe and aesthetically pleasing condition. Since trees in towns and cities are valuable assets and generally difficult to replace readily, the tree maintenance practices described here, including proper training and pruning, will often have an application in an urban environment. However, it should be recognised that many plants will not require some or all of these maintenance procedures.

Safe and healthy trees are desirable in urban streets, parks and gardens, while in natural woodlands, damaged and dead trees, as well as healthy ones, are important as many birds and small animals require tree hollows and dead trees for habitats. Dead and decaying trees are also hosts for insects, fungi, bacteria and other micro-organisms. In these situations, tree maintenance practices normally used in urban trees are not desirable, for example, the treatment of dead wood and hollow branches in farmlands and forest reserves could greatly upset the balance of nature. Thus it is readily demonstrated that trees are vital resources that must be protected.

One example of what can be done to recognise and protect important trees is the Register of Significant Trees run by the National Trust of Australia (Victoria) and the Royal Botanic Gardens, Melbourne. In this program, significant trees are registered in one or more categories and the owners are encouraged and advised to maintain these trees in a safe, healthy and attractive state, thus prolonging their survival. Trees are selected for this scheme by assessment of the following:

- horticultural or genetic value
- unique location or context
- localised distribution or rarity in cultivation
- age
- size
- aesthetic significance
- unusual form
- historical significance
- Aboriginal significance and
- outstanding example of species.

Many local councils also issue tree preservation orders which are an acknowledgement of the value of trees to the community.

At times it may be necessary to place a monetary value on a tree, for example, when such a valuation is required in compensation cases involving legal action. There are a number of systems employed to calculate the financial value of a tree. Some of these are listed in 'References and further reading' under 'Amenity tree valuation'. Most amenity tree valuations include a basic factor for size, plus modification for tree health, location, species, rarity, etc.

Tree growth and development

Some important features of tree growth and development are described below, including root and shoot extension, growth in diameter and branching. Knowledge of these is a prerequisite for understanding certain principles of tree care described in this text.

Root and shoot extension

The elongation and extension of plant roots and shoots takes place in small areas of the plant known as **meristems** which are found in the tips of roots and shoots. The actively dividing meristematic cells cause the root or shoot to elongate and, with maturity, the new cells differentiate into specialised vascular and cortex tissues.

As root meristem cells are quite delicate they are protected by a root cap

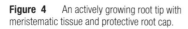

zone of cell differentiation

root hairs

zone of cell elongation

zone of frequent cell division

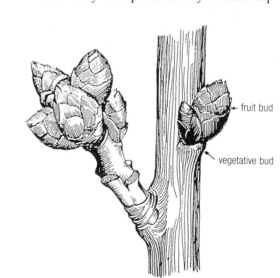

fruit bud

vegetative bud

Figure 4 An actively growing root tip with meristematic tissue and protective root cap.

Figure 5 Buds with a protective covering of scale leaves.

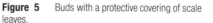

which repeatedly wears away as the root extends, producing a lubricant that assists movement of the root through the soil. The meristem produces new cells for the replacement of spent root-cap cells.

Modified scale leaves protect the meristematic cells found at the tips and intervals along the length of shoots. These scale leaves are arranged in structures knows as **buds**, which contain not only meristematic tissue, but also immature undeveloped leaves, shoots and/or flowers.

Growth in diameter

Growth in diameter is a feature of plant growth, but it is particularly marked in large woody plants such as trees. Actively dividing cells of the **cambium** are the primary sources of this growth.

In most vascular plants (other than monocotyledons) the **phloem** and **xylem** are separated by a vascular cambium layer. This microscopically thin area of actively dividing cells is responsible for the production of new phloem and xylem cells.

Cells produced on the inside of the cambium become xylem elements or wood; those produced on the outside become phloem elements, sometimes referred to as **bast**. Eventually, when these phloem cells die, they become cork or bark.

Initial woody stem growth results from the formation of a continuous cambium that joins all the vascular bundles that were separate in the young, soft herbaceous stem. Eventually, all the vascular bundles will also join. Thereafter, this secondary growth results in the formation of **wood** and **bark**.

In many woody plants the production of bark is not solely due to the formation and resultant death of phloem tissue. Many species also have the capacity to produce **cork cambium**, a second layer of meristematic tissue outside the phloem, which is responsible for the formation of cork or bark. This is particularly necessary in trees with large trunk diameters as the generally tough and unpalatable bark waterproofs and protects the stem against many of the ravages of pests, disease and the environment.

A tree growing in a temperate region usually produces one **annual ring** of wood growth per year. Such growth rings can be seen on a felled tree trunk as the alternation of lighter coloured spring wood with darker winter wood. The phenomenon is due to cells of the winter wood being smaller and denser than those of the spring wood. Cells produced in the spring are larger in order to cope with the transportation of the tree's greater requirement for water and minerals during this period of active growth. Generally, in tropical areas, trees continue to grow throughout the year, and thus fail to produce annual growth rings.

In some trees, the xylem cells become darker and heavier with age. Due to impregnation with lignin, tannins and resins the cells become stronger, more supportive, less porous, more durable and non-conductive. These cells, commonly referred to as **heartwood** cells, are considered to be physiologically inactive, but they can respond to wounding. The outer, actively conducting xylem elements are referred to as **sapwood**.

Branching

The attachment of branches is also an important element of tree growth. A good understanding of how branches are connected, and *not* connected, to trunks is essential for correct training, pruning and bracing of trees. This knowledge is also required by arborists when assessing the structural integrity or safety of trees. It is also basic to understanding the movement of pathogens in trees and this, in turn, relates to the management of diseases and to cavity treatment.

It is unfortunate that this topic has generally been either misunderstood or ignored in most resource material available to arborists. What has been most damaging to trees is the coincidence of this lack of understanding with the development of very efficient tree pruning tools such as the chainsaw. This situation has resulted in a great deal of damage being done to trees in the name of 'pruning', with the possibility that every cut may inflict a serious wound.

The fundamentals of correct pruning were well known and documented over a century ago and, recently, the research findings of Dr A.L. Shigo and co-workers in the United States have become available. This new work verifies and extends the advice given in some of the older sources. These notes on branch attachment summarise some of these findings. Readers are also referred to Dr Shigo's books and published papers for detailed treatment of this subject, and much other valuable information besides. Some of his publications are listed in 'References and further reading' under 'Arboriculture tree surgery/pruning/tree care'.

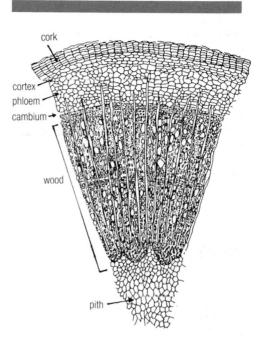

Figure 6   Transverse section of a two-year-old apple stem.

Branch development

In each growing season, branch growth usually begins before trunk growth. Shigo describes a 'downward wave' of growth, beginning with bud activity at the branch tips, followed by division of the vascular cambium from the branch tips downwards, with the vascular cambium of the trunk and, finally, of the supporting roots developing later in the season.

Where the newly developing branch xylem tissues meet the trunk, they turn sharply downwards to produce a collar around the base of the branch, the **branch collar**. Figure 8a. Later, as branch growth slows down, trunk growth speeds up — with trunk tissue then growing over the branch collar to produce a **trunk collar**. Figure 8b.

This annual build-up of trunk collar over branch collar holds the branch on to the trunk, like a series of ball and socket connections overlaid on each other. Figures 8c and 8d. Note that there is not a

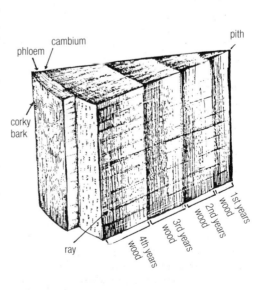

Figure 7   Section of a mature woody stem.

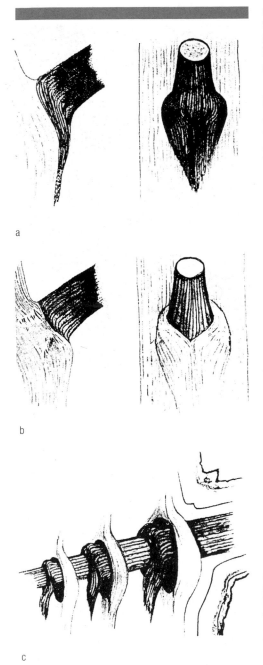

a

b

c

direct connection of xylem tissue except for the small strip of xylem leading *down* from the branch collar. In this way the branch is 'held on' to the trunk, yet partly separate from it.

Branch protection features

On the upper side of the branch–trunk union, the branch cambium and trunk cambium develop in different directions. Because the xylem cells produced in this area have no room for expansion, a zone of compacted wood develops internally between branch and trunk. This zone is indicated externally by the **branch bark ridge**, which is formed by the bark cells compacting and erupting outwards. The branch bark ridge shows permanently on the trunk and is an important guide for correct pruning.

The zone of compacted xylem in the upper junction of branch and trunk is an important **protection zone** which resists the spread of pathogens from branch to trunk, and vice versa. Another protection zone forms at the junction of branch pith and trunk pith, the pith protection

Figure 8 Trunk and branch collar development.
a Branch collar development.
b Trunk collar development.
c and **d** Interlocking arrangement of branch and trunk collars.

d

zone, and consists of thicker walled cells containing anti-microbial substances.

When branches die, break, or are pruned off, another protection zone begins to form in the branch base. This is a chemical boundary produced *in response* by the tree. This zone resists the spread of decay organisms into the branch base, while allowing the 'unwanted' branch to be digested and shed. This system of natural boundaries involves an interaction between the tree and its associated micro-organisms; the tree provides a food source for micro-organisms which in turn, participate in the shedding of unhealthy or failed parts by the tree. The success of this system depends on the tree's capacity to wall off such parts from healthy tissue. This system will fail if the protection zones are weak or disrupted, or if an attacking pathogen is very strong. Such a situation may be predisposed by stress, genetic factors, or by making pruning cuts which disrupt the natural protection zones.

As a branch begins to die or slows its growth, the trunk collar at the branch base becomes more distinct. This clearly indicates the correct location for a pruning cut 'at the junction of each branch to the stem there is a swell or bulge, and the branch should be removed close to the outside of it' (Grigor 1868). This author also cautions against the 'evil consequences' of flush cuts and resultant trunk decay.

After the branch dies, a callus collar will form. The callus collar is roughly circular in shape and will usually close the wound after the branch has been shed. When pruning dead branches, the **callus collar** must not be damaged or removed as this will lead to infection and decay of trunk tissue above and below the wound.

Problems of growth

Co-dominant stems (double leaders) Not all 'branches' are true branches; where two trunk stems, co-dominant stems, arise at one point (sometimes referred to as a 'V-crotch'), each will have a direct

Figure 9   Co-dominant stem with included bark.

connection with the trunk below. In this situation there are no collars or normal branch protection features to resist the spread of infection into the trunk xylem other than the usual Wall 1 of CODIT, a vertical plugging of xylem vessels (described under 'Compartmentalisation of decay' below). A **stem bark ridge** will form between the two trunks and this should be used as a pruning guide if one stem is to be removed.

A correct pruning cut will start just outside the stem bark ridge at the top and intersect a point on the trunk adjacent to the lowest point of the ridge.

Included bark This may be described as an ingrowing or inturned branch bark ridge. If something disrupts the normal pattern of cambial development, preventing normal branch attachment from occurring, there will be no interlocking branch and trunk collars. This creates a weak structure, with the expanding

Figure 10   Poorly attached branch with included bark.

trunk and branch being separated from each other by bark. Co-dominant stems can also develop with included bark. Pruning of stems and branches with included bark is the same as for true branches and double leaders with up-turned bark ridges.

Stems and branches with included bark should be pruned out as soon as possible in the life of a tree. Trees which habitually produce many such unions should be removed and replaced wherever possible.

Compartmentalisation of decay

Trees are naturally shedding plants. Non-woody parts such as leaves, flowers, bark, fruit and absorbing roots are continually being shed. This shedding process involves the setting of **boundaries** such as the abscission zone

when leaves are shed and the root periderms when absorbing roots are shed.

In the woody parts of the plants, as a response to wounding and infection by pathogens, existing boundaries are strengthened and new boundaries are created. The **pre-set boundaries** exist because trees grow as compartmented plants. In the tree trunk these compartments are formed by late wood cells at the outer margin of each growth increment and sheets of xylem ray cells.

The **new boundaries** formed by the plant in response to wounding are

- plugging of xylem vessels with extractives to resist vertical spread of pathogens, and
- a barrier zone of protective cells formed by the vascular tissue after wounding.

These functions have been described by Shigo and co-workers (Shigo 1977,1987) as the 'CODIT system' — compartmentalisation of decay in trees.

The walls of CODIT represent the naturally occurring boundaries within woody stems, but should not be construed as actual anatomical features. In general, the walls of CODIT resist rather than stop the spread of decay. The CODIT model consists of two parts:

Part A: Walls 1, 2 and 3 (the reaction zone) and

Part B: Wall 4 (the barrier zone)

Wall 1 resists vertical spread of decay; the weakest wall of part A. Wall 2 resists inward spread of decay. Wall 3 resists radial spread of decay; the strongest wall of part A. Wall 4 separates wood present at the time of wounding from wood formed after wounding; the strongest wall of CODIT.

The walls of the reaction zone may confine decay to a small area within a stem, or decay may spread to all wood present at the time of wounding. The ability of trees to compartmentalise decay varies between species and even within a species. Other factors involved include pathogen virulence, tree vigour and the effects of further wounding. The barrier zone is usually effective in con-

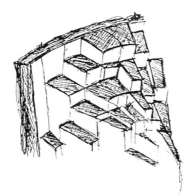

wall 1

a

wall 2

b

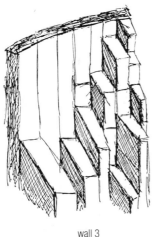

wall 3

c

wall 4 (barrier zone)

d

fining decay to wood present at the time of wounding.

Decay can spread to new wood if the barrier zone is breached. Consequently, it is essential that arborists be aware of the possible consequences of inflicting further wounds upon the tree, especially when pruning, bracing and treating cavities.

Figure 11   Compartmentalisation of decay in trees
a CODIT wall 1 (cross hatched)   Plugging of xylom cells resist vertical spread of decay.
b CODIT wall 2 (cross hatched)   Latewood cells at the outer margin of each growth increment resist inward spread of decay.
c CODIT wall 3 (cross hatched)   Vascular rays resist radial spread of decay.
d CODIT wall 4 (shaded)   Barrier zone, formed by the vascular cambium after wounding.

Tree planting and establishment

The planting of trees suitable for particular situations and purposes is to be commended and encouraged. Trees are becoming a rapidly dwindling resource. However, tree planting is recognised as being absolutely essential in many districts, particularly for the control of soil degradation. A number of practical considerations should be taken into account when planting and establishing trees. Some of these are discussed below, but specialised techniques such as transplanting established trees, direct seeding and landscape construction are beyond the scope of this text.

Selection of suitable species

Before planting a tree it is most important that an appropriate species is chosen for the site, and that this specimen will grow and perform as required. The choice of species is wide so it is wise to consider those that have already proved to be successful growers in the same area.

In recent years it has been popular to plant native species. Although indigenous plants (particularly those raised from local seed sources) are often preferred, exotic species — both evergreen and deciduous — may also be worthy of consideration. Although evergreens remain in leaf all year, they do not provide the colourful autumn foliage often associated with deciduous trees like maples (*Acer* spp.) and sweet gums (*Liquidambar* spp.).

A number of trees are also grown for their spectacular flowers; examples include Bull Bay Magnolia (*Magnolia grandiflora*) and Firewheel Tree (*Stenocarpus sinuatus*). Leaf texture may also be considered when selecting species, for instance, the leaves of the Wych Elm (*Ulmus glabra*) are coarsely textured, whereas those of Flaxleaf Paperbark (*Melaleuca linariifolia*) are quite fine. Many trees are also noted for their fruit, which may be soft and colourful, such as those of Persimmon (*Diospyros kaki*), or woody but interesting like those of banksias (*Banksia* spp.).

Many trees have other desirable qualities. Some have interesting trunks, such as the birches (*Betula* spp.). Others have attractive bark; the paperbarks (*Melaleuca* spp.) being a good example. Some, including the Native Frangipani (*Hymenosporum flavum*), produce perfumed flowers while others, like the Lemon-scented Gum (*Eucalyptus citriodora*), have aromatic foliage.

However, some also have properties considered to be undesirable. These include 'limb droppers', of which River Red Gum (*Eucalyptus camaldulensis*) is one example. Some trees drop dangerously large fruit; the Bunya Bunya Pine (*Araucaria bidwillii*) is renowned for dropping large cones up to 200 mm in diameter and weighing 5–6 kg. Trees which can cause poisoning, injury or irritation should also be used with caution, particularly in areas frequented by small children; examples of these are the Pyramid Tree (*Lagunaria patersonia*) which produces seed cases that cause skin irritation and

Figure 12   Red Ironbark (*Eucalyptus sideroxylon*), a tree with interesting deeply furrowed, dark bark.

Figure 13   London Plane Trees (*Platanus × acerifolia*). Excellent deciduous shade trees.

White Cedar (*Melia azederach*) which has poisonous seeds. Suckering plants, which include poplars (*Populus* spp.) and elms (*Ulmus* spp.), can also cause nuisance problems.

It is also essential that the species chosen are tolerant of local environmental conditions. From district to district soils can vary in salinity, fertility, drainage and ability to retain water. Similarly, climatic factors including rainfall, wind and temperature may vary. Tolerance of coastal conditions or pollution may also influence plant selection.

Trees may also be selected for their ability to fulfil particular purposes which include windbreaks, bird attraction, hedging, screening, shade and control of soil salinity. In bushfire-prone areas it is desirable to consider planting shields of trees with fire-retardant properties. These plants normally have a high moisture content and include Kurrajong (*Brachychiton populneus*) and Peppercorn Tree (*Schinus molle*).

Other criteria worthy of consideration in the selection of species include factors associated with the site. The presence of overhead power and telephone lines can influence the maximum height of species to be chosen. Leaking underground drains and sewerage lines may also cause problems as they can become fouled by plant roots in search of water, especially in drought conditions.

Thought should be given to the form, ultimate height and spread of a species. In the case of large spreading trees, such as Moreton Bay Fig (*Ficus macrophylla*) and oaks (*Quercus* spp.), space is required for these trees to grow to their full size and beauty. Too often large trees of the bush and open spaces are planted in unsuitable situations, including under powerlines, in small gardens or beside buildings. Although these trees often look most attractive when young, when older they prove to be nuisances in restricted situations. Such plantings can lead to many problems, increasing the risk of fire, and cause drying and shrinkage of certain clay soils leading to cracking of building walls. Although there have been no recorded instances of damage to properly constructed concrete slabs, other types of foundation may be affected. Ultimate removal of trees can be an expensive process, especially if large branches overhang adjacent buildings. In particular, inappropriate plantings of Blue Gum (*Eucalyptus globulus*) and Southern Mahogany (*Eucalyptus botryoides*) have caused much concern recently. Further it should be noted that where some large trees have been removed, heaving of the soil has resulted because of increased soil moisture.

For further assistance in the selection of species, various references are listed under 'Selection of trees' in 'References and further reading'.

Selection of plant material

Selected plants should be healthy, vigorous and correctly labelled. When purchasing planting material, the extra cost of purchasing advanced plants may be of little advantage as young plants generally adjust readily and make up for the difference in size.

Of prime importance in the selection of stock is ensuring that plants are not root-bound or weak and spindly. Evidence of a root-bound condition is the presence of girdling roots. Advanced plants growing in small containers are often root-bound. Constricted roots may be seen growing above the soil level and through drainage holes at the base of the container. Such plants should be avoided.

Preparation of the planting site

Successful tree establishment may be promoted by thoroughly preparing the site well before planting.

Weeds should be controlled in good time for planting. Where perennial hard-to-kill weeds, such as Couch (*Cynodon dactylon*), are a problem, they should be treated, preferably while still actively growing, with a translocated herbicide such as glyphosate.

When planting ornamental trees it is absolutely essential to allow adequate space for the tree to develop and achieve its full potential. The growth of other plants, including other trees, in competition with a newly planted tree is undesirable. In order to allow adequate light and space for full development, the branches of neighbouring trees may be pruned selectively.

The addition of humus to the soil is helpful in improving its structure. It is also beneficial to incorporate coarse sand in heavy clay soils, and to deep rip them to shatter the subsoil. A disturbed subsoil should improve movement of water and enhance root growth, but lessen the possibility of waterlogging.

In wet situations, consideration should be given to providing suitable surface and subsurface drainage.

It is normally appropriate to make each planting hole about twice as wide as the container or root system.

Transportation of planting stock

Trees, whether containerised or bare-rooted, should be transported under cover from the nursery to the planting site. Container stock should be thoroughly watered prior to transportation. Bare-rooted stock should have the root system covered in wet hessian or similar material. Exposure to the high winds experienced during transportation, even for short distances, will cause desiccation of the foliage and exposed roots. Obviously, transportation over long distances will increase the chance of damage to the plants unless proper care is taken to protect them. Stock should be planted with minimum delay on arrival at the site and ideally only sufficient numbers taken for each day's planting. If storage is required on site, then bare-rooted plants will need to be heeled in and an adequate watering regime established for all plants.

Time of planting

Tree planting is generally undertaken during the cooler months after the first rains have fallen. In districts that experience severe frosts, planting may take place in early spring when the risk of frosts has lessened. Container- or tube-grown plants may be planted at any time of the year, so long as sufficient care is given to the trees after planting. Deciduous, bare-rooted stock should only be planted in winter when dormant.

Planting

Plants should be kept moist prior to planting, particularly container-grown or tube-grown stock, making them easier to remove and plant out from containers.

To dislodge container-grown trees from tubes or pots, the pots may be up-ended and the plants gently knocked out. Stock grown in perforated plastic tubes can be removed by simply tearing a strip from each tube. With veneer-tube-grown stock, it is necessary to remove rubber bands from the tubes, then partially unwrap the veneer. The process is often completed in the planting hole by pulling the tube up and away from the plant while it is surrounded by loose soil.

Any bound roots should be gently teased out and girdling, damaged or broken roots trimmed with sharp secateurs prior to planting. Roots should be encouraged to grow outwards and downwards. For bare-rooted stock, a mound may be formed in the planting hole over which roots can be spread.

Trees should be planted no deeper than the junction of the roots and the stem or the soil level of the container.

a

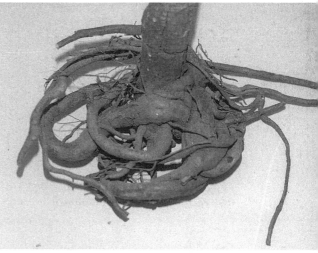

b

Figure 14 **a** A girdling root on a mature tree. The planting of pot-bound nursery stock **b** or failing to tease roots at planting time can result in this condition.

Burial of the stem may result in collar rot and death of the plant.

To eliminate air pockets about the root system, the planting hole should be back-filled with soil free from large lumps, which can then be consolidated lightly. Finally, the plant must be watered in well. A shallow basin around the tree will enable easier watering. In areas which are

• for *support* of newly planted trees in windy locations or advanced nursery transplants which have a large crown volume in relation to the size of the root ball; or
• for *protection* of young trees from mowers, cars and people.

Should it be necessary to stake a tree, the stakes should be placed in the ground prior to planting. Trees should not be tied rigidly as this will inhibit the movement necessary to promote sound growth, and will also lead to damage of the bark and trunk. Preferably, two stakes should be

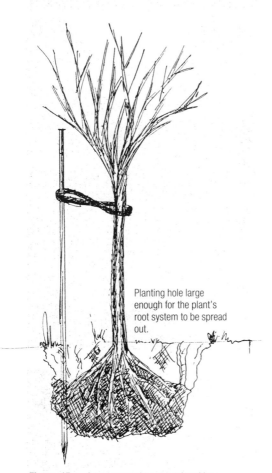

Planting hole large enough for the plant's root system to be spread out.

Figure 15   A tree secured to one stake with a 'figure-of-eight' tie.

damp or have a high watertable, it may be advisable to plant trees in mounds raised above the natural ground level in order to improve surface drainage but, if suitable plant species have been selected for the site, this should not be necessary. Any soil imported for building mounds should be blended with the earth dug from the site.

Staking

Where possible, trees should not be staked as this practice can retard the development of a sound and stable trunk and root system. However, staking may be necessary:

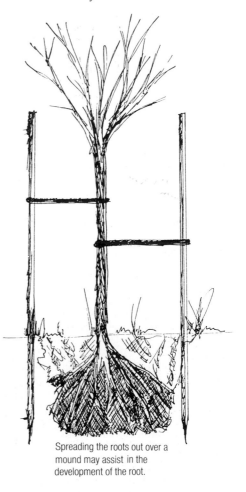

Spreading the roots out over a mound may assist in the development of the root.

Figure 16   A deciduous bare-rooted tree planted in a well prepared planting hole on an internal mound and supported by webbing to two stakes.

used and these should be placed on either side of the tree, at right angles to the direction of the prevailing wind. When using only one stake, this is normally placed on the windward side of the tree, but not so close to the tree that it causes it to grow away from the stake.

The material used for tying should not cause injury to the trunk and a range of different ties may be used. Strips of terylene webbing or rubber, approximately 25–50 mm wide, may be used on young trees. Wire, string and similar non-elastic materials should *not* be used. In the case of advanced trees requiring guying, the guy cables may be secured to the tree with eyeleted terylene webbing slings.

Ties should be placed only as high as is necessary to provide suitable support. Ties placed too high can create too much support and result in weak growth. Conversely, ties placed too low may provide insufficient support and cause damage to the trunk. Factors that should be considered in determining the most suitable position for tying include stem diameter, stem taper, tree height and species. It is essential to check plant ties regularly to ensure damage is not caused to the tree. These ties should be removed as soon as the tree is self-supporting.

Formative pruning

Formative pruning is carried out to develop a sound, safe tree, consistent with the natural growth habit of the species.

Where the root system of a tree is small in relation to its framework, judicious pruning should lessen the stress of transpiration loss during transplanting and establishment. When required, the effect should be achieved by thinning no more than 25% of the crown volume. Thinning more than 25% of the crown volume would result in a severe depletion of stored plant sugars, leading to stunted growth.

Dead, diseased and damaged branches must be removed during formative pruning. Poorly placed and crossing branches should also be removed to improve the structure and prevent rubbing and limb damage. Any suckers and

a

b

Figure 17　**a** and **b** An advanced transplant guyed with eyeleted webbing slings to three stakes.

a

b

Figure 18   a and **b** Treatment of a co-dominant
stem during formative pruning.

undesirable rootstock growths can also be eliminated.

In developing a strong trunk and framework, the occurrence of weak forks must be avoided. The weakest crotch is one that forks into two leaders of about the same diameter; this is known as a co-dominant stem or 'V-crotch'. In the mature tree, such a crotch is liable to split into two, resulting in possible damage to people and property. This split leaves the remaining portion of the tree severely weakened and unsightly in appearance, as well as creating a large wound prone to decay. It is essential that co-dominant stems are treated during formative pruning, allowing growth to continue as one leader rather than two.

Attention should also be given to branches with steep angles of attachment and no branch-bark ridge present at the upper junction of the fork. These will have bark-included forks. Early removal of these formations is recommended as this lack of connecting wood or true branch collar will result in permanent weakness at that point.

When pruning to direct future growth, vigorous laterals may be shortened back in relation to main leaders. Where possible, the main leader or leaders should generally be left *unpruned*. The retention of terminal buds on leaders will suppress growth below the bud and invigorate the leader, **apical dominance**. It has also been found that removal of terminals will retard root growth until new terminals are formed. This may be injurious to newly planted trees.

All laterals on the young tree may be regarded as temporary, being progressively pruned off over several seasons, up to the selected *lowest permanent branch*. Temporary laterals arising from the trunk are retained both to protect the trunk and to strengthen it, by adding to girth growth and stem taper. Over-vigorous growth can be shortened to reduce competition with the top.

Thoughtful formative pruning in the early post-planting years should eliminate the need for making large pruning wounds to trees in later life. The result will be stronger, safer, healthier and better looking trees which cost far less to maintain. Reference to 'Problems of growth' in the chapter 'Tree growth and development' is suggested for a deeper understanding of pruning principles. See also the chapters 'Pruning' and 'Branch and tree removal'.

Fertilising

Fertilisers and composted manures may be applied at planting time to provide plant nutrients. The materials selected and rates of application will depend on the type and size of tree planted, as well as on the properties of the soil. Generally, complete fertilisers are used but, to avoid burning the roots by direct contact, the fertiliser should be mixed into the surface of the soil. Subsequent waterings will leach it down into the root zone.

Watering

Following planting, it is critical that trees be given a thorough, deep watering to consolidate soil around the roots, eliminate air pockets, and prevent drying of the root system.

The need for further watering will be influenced by a number of factors including climate, plant species, and soil type. Supplementary watering during the first year of growth will be beneficial in the establishment of street and parkland trees.

Mulching

Materials such as leaf mould and straw, or even crushed rock, coarse sand and wood chips, may be used to cover the soil about the newly planted tree. Mulching is most advisable since it minimises soil moisture loss resulting from evaporation and should reduce growth of many weeds. It must be stressed that mulch material *should not be piled against the tree stem*, as this provides an ideal environment for the development of fungi (for example, those causing collar rot) and a habitat for pests.

Ideally, organic mulch materials should not be used until they are at least partially decomposed. Fresh organic material may contain toxins which could leach into the soil, and its decomposition could result in a temporary deficiency of nitrogen.

Tree protection

A range of materials is available for protecting trees from damage. The type and extent of protection will be influenced by a number of factors including situation, tree size, and aesthetics.

A stout stake or two is normally all that is needed to provide some protection for the newly planted tree. However, robust and aesthetically acceptable tree guards may be more desirable in areas frequented by vandals, vehicles, and animals.

Although the cost of tree guards can be high, so is the cost of replacing badly

Figure 19   A robust tree guard for protection from vandals and motor vehicles of a newly planted street tree.

damaged young trees. The capital cost of constructing sound reusable tree guards should be more than offset by the cost of plants and labour in the tree replacement programs.

Over-protection of newly planted trees from prevailing winds will be detrimental to trunk and root development. Therefore, wind permeability should be a consideration when designing tree guards. Wire mesh guards are useful in protecting small young trees from vermin such as rabbits in areas not subject to traffic. Punched polythene sheeting can also be used in these areas to provide additional protection from high winds. These polythene guards also cause condensation of water on their inside surfaces, thus reducing desiccation and encouraging growth. The trunks of taller planting stock can be protected from vermin by flexible, heavyweight wraps.

Durable, robust guards made from metal, timber and recycled plastic are widely used for protecting amenity trees from vehicles. Surrounding environments, such as streetscapes or heritage areas, should influence the style and design.

Aftercare

Post-planting care is an essential requirement of any tree planting program. In particular, it is of utmost importance that trees be watered during dry periods, at least until established. Attention should also be given to weed and disease control, mulching and pruning.

Tree planting programs should be planned in accordance with resources and labour available for post-planting care. It is false economy to plant large numbers of trees only to have a large percentage die through lack of follow-up maintenance.

Tree inspection

Tree inspections are fundamental to any tree management operation. Before any work on a tree is initiated it must be inspected. Such an inspection may be informal or formal, but it should assess the condition of the tree and recommend the extent and type of work required. Thorough assessment, especially in large trees, will often require the tree to be climbed.

It is not always possible to select an ideal time of year for a tree inspection, but it is desirable to inspect deciduous trees in leaf so that dead, diseased and dying branches can be readily detected. At this time any problems that produce foliar symptoms should also be easily seen. Deciduous trees should *also* be inspected after leaf fall when structural weaknesses and cavities may more easily be observed. Evergreen trees can be inspected at any time of year.

Tree inspection should begin by looking at the most obvious above-ground parts such as leaves, fruit, branch system and trunk. Inspection can also continue downwards from the base of the tree to the root system and soil. It could also include an investigation into the history of drainage, excavations and soil movements on the site. Testing of soil, plant tissues and decay may also be undertaken if it is considered to be necessary.

Some details of common tree problems and their symptoms are given in the table below.

Where a number of trees are inspected on a more widespread and formal scale such inspections are often referred to as 'tree surveys'.

TREE INSPECTION DATA COLLECTION SHEET

Location : _____   Tree no. : _____

Arboricultural details

Botanical name : _____   Date planted : _____

Height : _____   Girth : _____   Canopy width : _____

Age : Immature _____ Semi-mature _____ Mature _____ Over-mature _____

Condition : Good _____ Fair _____ Poor _____ Dead _____

Recommendations for work required

Staking : _____ Mulching : _____ Fertilizing : _____ Stake removal : _____

Pruning : Formative pruning _____ Cleaning out _____ Crown thinning _____

Crown reduction _____ Crown lifting _____ Crown renewal _____

Wound treatment : _____ Cavity treatment : _____ Bracing : _____

Branch removal : _____ Tree removal : _____ Stump removal : _____

Sucker/Seedling control : _____ Weed control : _____

Pest/Disease control : _____ Soil aeration : _____

Comments : _____

Priority : Urgent _____ High _____ Medium _____ Low _____

Surrounding features

Position of tree : _____

Root width : _____ Footpath width : _____ Nature-strip width : _____

Location of underground services : _____

Location of above-ground services : _____

Problems caused by tree : _____

Adjacent buildings : _____

Significance/Amenity value

Horticultural value : _____ Age : _____ Size : _____ Form : _____

Historic significance : _____ Rarity in cultivation : _____

Unique location/context : _____

Further details : _____

Name of Inspector : _____ Date : _____

Figure 20   Example of street tree survey sheet.

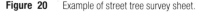

The success of tree surveys is dependent upon the objectives of the survey and detailed, accurate information recording. Systems that can contribute to recording survey information are tree numbering systems, survey maps, and data collection sheets.

A satisfactory result from any tree survey will not be achieved unless information can be readily retrieved. Such information should include the survey recommendations which are particularly important for arborists carrying out any resultant tree maintenance. Although computers can be of value for storing and retrieving survey data, a simple card or book system may be more practical, especially for field workers.

Table 1   Common problem conditions and some possible causes

Conditions	Possible causes
Leaf problems	
Abnormal colour and small size	Nutritional disorders
	Vascular/root problems
	Waterlogging
	Pests (5)
	Diseases (3)
	Genetic abnormalities
Mosaics, yellows, ringspots	Diseases (3)
Leaf spots, scabs	Diseases (1,2)
Rusts, mildews, leafcurls	Diseases (1)
Malformation	Pests (5)
	Diseases (1)
	Genetic abnormalities
Galls	Pests (5,6)
	Diseases (1,2)
Wilting	Drought stress
	Vascular/root problems
	Pests (5)
	Diseases (1,2,3)
Dead tissue	High soil salts
	Diseases
	Nutritional disorders
Tissue loss	Pests (6)
	Diseases (1,2)
Early leaf fall/loss	Drought stress
	Pests (5,6)
	Diseases (1,2,4)
	Waterlogging
	Vascular/root problems
	Underground gas leakage
	Chemical poisoning
	High soil salts
Branch, trunk, twig and shoot problems	
Stunted growth	Nutritional disorders
	Chemical poisoning
	Drought stress
	Pests (5,6,7)
	Diseases (1,2,3,4)
Bark loss/holes	Pests (6)
	Diseases (1,2)

Dieback	Soil salting
	Chemical poisoning
	Pests (6)
	Diseases (1)
Poor structure	Co-dominant stems
	Weak branch attachments
	Heavy horizontal limbs
	Cavities
	Crossing and poorly placed limbs
Mechanical/	'Lopping and topping'
human damage	'Flush cutting'
	Branch 'stumps and stubs'
	Machinery misuse

Root system problems

Loss/lack of feeder roots	Waterlogging
	Poor soil aeration
	Poor drainage
	Soil compaction
	Pests (6,7)
	Diseases (1)
	Machinery
Galls	Diseases (1)

1 Fungi
2 Bacteria
3 Virus and virus like pathogens
4 Parasitic flowering plants
5 Sucking pests
6 Chewing/boring pests
7 Nematodes

Pruning

Pruning involves the selective removal of plant material, particularly branches. Although not always required by all trees, pruning is an important practice in the management of amenity trees. Where required, pruning should begin in the nursery.

Details of techniques and principles of pruning for amenity purposes are set out below. Before reading this chapter refer to the chapter 'Tree growth and development'. Formative pruning is referred to on page 15 under 'Tree planting and establishment'. Techniques used in pruning large limbs are discussed in the chapter 'Branch and tree removal'.

Reasons for pruning

Ornamental trees may be pruned for any of a number of reasons, which may affect the health, safety and aesthetic appearance of a tree. Some reasons for pruning are:

- to compensate for root loss;
- to influence plant form;
- to remove dead, diseased and damaged wood;
- to remove crossing, rubbing wood;
- to eliminate structural weaknesses such as co-dominant stems and poorly attached limbs;
- to reduce the damage that could result from strong winds, storms and snow, or to repair such damage;
- to improve the quality or production of flowers and fruit;
- to encourage and stimulate the production of new wood;
- to eliminate undesirable growth from suckers or rootstocks;
- to improve access and/or views under the canopy;

- to admit more air and light into and through the canopy; and
- to modify the width and/or height of a tree.

Timing of pruning

Most trees may be pruned at any time of year without ill effect, but it should be noted that pruning of some types of trees, especially deciduous trees, in late summer is sometimes detrimental. This can induce late-season growth from next season's buds which may then be damaged by cold temperatures in winter. Among deciduous species, birches (*Betula* spp.) and maples (*Acer* spp.) are known to exude sap or 'bleed' profusely when pruned from mid-winter to late spring. Therefore, it is generally thought desirable to prune these trees in summer, when in full leaf, or just after leaf fall. Walnuts, (*Juglans* spp.) are normally best pruned when in full leaf during summer, as profuse 'bleeding' will occur if pruning is carried out at any other time.

The possibility of diseases infecting pruning cuts may also influence the time of pruning. For instance, the Apricot (*Prunus armeniaca*) is susceptible to Eutypa dieback and is normally pruned in the middle of winter. At this time, spore discharge of the fungus *Eutypa armeniacae* is generally at its lowest level.

Deciduous trees should *not* be pruned when leaves are forming or falling because less energy is available for defence of wounds; it is best to prune late in the dormant season or after leaves are fully formed (Shigo 1986).

For aesthetic reasons, free-flowering ornamental plants should not be pruned before they have finished flowering. Many flowering ornamental plants are pruned on an annual basis to stimulate flower production. Plants which flower on new wood (the current season's growth), such as Crepe Myrtle (*Lagerstroemia indica*), are pruned in winter; spring flowering plants that bloom predominantly on one-year-old wood (last season's growth), such as many *Prunus* spp., are pruned after flowering. This practice directs growth into fewer shoots and not into fruit, thereby assisting in the development of strong growth for future flower production.

For practical purposes, it may be more convenient to carry out some pruning operations at certain times of the year. For instance in the case of deciduous ornamental trees, pruning to provide views and access beneath the canopy should be carried out when the tree is in full leaf. At this time, the base of the canopy is at its lowest level above the ground, and a more precise job may be carried out. Similarly, dead wood is easier to locate in deciduous trees when in full leaf, although working in the canopy at this time may not necessarily be convenient. However, pruning of plane trees, (*Platanus* spp.) is normally best done when they are totally leafless in winter, as 'hair-like' fibres on young leaves can cause respiratory problems in some people.

Pruning technique

A selection of tools may be used for pruning and the choice depends on the size and location of the wood to be removed. This includes various types of secateurs and saws.

Where secateurs are used, these may have a blade that cuts to one side of the anvil. These usually have a 'parrot beak' or hook-shaped blade and anvil; when used with the cutting blade closest to the main part of the plant, these secateurs will cause minimal bruising. When using secateurs, cutting should require less effort if the branch being pruned is gently eased towards the anvil of the secateurs, opening up the cut.

a

b

c

Figure 21   **a** Pruning a lateral to a bud.
b Pruning a branch to a lateral.
c Pruning a lateral to its point of origin.

Generally, permanent branches should not be tip pruned or shortened. However, where pruning must be done for aesthetics and tree health, all pruning cuts should be made to growing points. When pruning a lateral to a bud, the final cut should be just above and at an angle away from the bud. When a branch is being shortened, the cut should be made to a healthy lateral, which should be no less than one-third of the diameter of the portion being removed. Removal of more than 25% of foliage from any branch will reduce its capacity for healthy growth and defence against disease.

Large limbs should be removed with a saw. It is important that these limbs be undercut during pruning to prevent tearing of bark and wood as the branch falls.

Heavy branches should be removed in sections to prevent damage to the tree and its surroundings. Small branch sections may be handheld by the operator and thrown clear, but larger sections may require the use of lowering ropes. These techniques are discussed in the chapter 'Branch and tree removal'.

When pruning, it is important not to leave stubs as they are unsightly, and they may also die back creating an entry point and food source for pests and diseases. Branches being removed entirely should be pruned to their point of origin.

Final cuts should be made to the outside of the branch collar. This may be recognised as a bulge or swelling of stem tissue around the butt of a branch. If the branch collar is not apparent, then the branch bark ridge may be used as a guide — by cutting outside it and angling the cut at an equal and opposite angle as illustrated. The branch bark ridge may be recognised as an area of raised bark on the upper side of the junction of a branch to a stem. Dead branches and stubs should be pruned to the outside of the (callus) collar.

These pruning directions are referred to by Dr A.L. Shigo as 'natural target pruning'. The first target being the branch collar and the second being the branch bark ridge.

Figure 22   Branch removal.
a Undercut — approximately one-third of branch diameter deep.
b Top cut — made approximately half of branch diameter further out from the trunk.
c Resultant small branch stub prior to the final cut.
d Final cut — to the outside of the branch collar.
e A branch removal operation in progress.

a

Pruning to these targets preserves the protection zones at the branch base, minimising the development of decay in the main stem and maximising the potential for compartmentalisation of the wound. (Refer to 'Tree growth and development' chapter).

In general, when pruning, the aim should be to make the smallest number of cuts of the smallest possible size.

It is now accepted that pruning cuts should not be painted with any kind of wound dressing. The best way to aid the trees defence is not to damage the natural protection zones when making pruning cuts.

Branch removal or pruning operations are potentially dangerous and should never be carried out without adequate safety measures. See the chapters 'Branch and tree removal' and 'Tree work procedures' for further details.

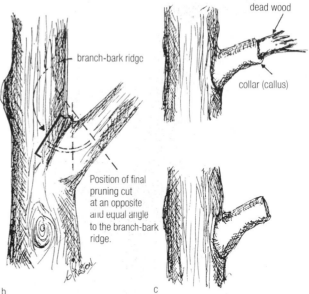

Figure 23   **a** Pruning a dead branch stub.
b Pruning of branch with no apparent collar.
c Pruning of a dead branch. Note that the collar must not be damaged — remove the dead wood only.

Types of pruning operation

Described below are some principal classes of pruning for mature ornamental trees. These are: cleaning out, crown thinning, crown reduction, crown lifting and crown renewal.

Cleaning out

Cleaning out is possibly the most common pruning operation carried out in mature ornamental trees. It includes

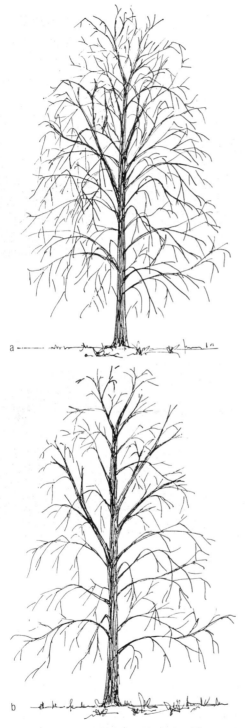

removal of dead, diseased, damaged, weak and crossing wood. Epicormic growths and watershoots may be removed but, in species where epicormic growths form part of the natural growth habit of the tree, such as elms (*Ulmus* spp.) and lindens (*Tillia* spp.), these should be retained.

Cleaning out should also entail the removal of foreign objects and climbing plants, such as Ivy (*Hedera* spp.). These plants compete with the tree for soil moisture, nutrients and sunlight and, by creating damp and shaded conditions around the trunk, they provide an ideal environment for insects and the growth of fungi. Climbing plants can also conceal structural problems, such as cavities, and they may become excessively heavy and cause limb breakage.

Crown thinning

Crown thinning involves reduction in density of the crown. This operation would not normally be carried out on conifers, so it is generally confined to deciduous broadleaf trees.

Trees may be crown thinned to reduce damage that could result from crown resistance to strong winds, storms and snow. Crown thinning may be carried out to admit more air and light into and through the canopy, thereby reducing the occurrence of certain pests and diseases, while also increasing light intensity for plants or people beneath the tree. In the case of transplanted trees, or trees with extensive root damage from excavations, compaction and so on, this procedure may be necessary to compensate for root loss.

Crown thinning should begin with cleaning out, unless this has been done beforehand. It is usual to confine most of the work to thinning the periphery of the crown, removing secondary branches only, and reducing the crown volume by no more than 25%. The operator normally begins at the top of the tree, working down and clearing prunings as work progresses. Both the size and number of wounds should be kept to a minimum.

Figure 24   Crown thinning **a** Before and **b** after thinning.

Excessive thinning in some species such as elms (*Ulmus* spp.) may stimulate epicormic activity on framework limbs, or may result in sunscald of thin-barked trees such as ashes (*Fraxinus* spp.).

As trees approach maturity, the ratio between the foliage (which supplies energy) and the wood mass of branches and stems becomes smaller, so that the removal of even small amounts of foliage may result in weakening and decline of branches.

Care, therefore, needs to be taken in mature trees not to overprune individual branches or the whole tree. In some cases, in order to preserve tree health, it may not be desirable to crown thin at all.

The final crown thinned 'product' should be balanced and consistent with the natural habit of the species.

Crown reduction

Crown reduction is also sometimes referred to as 'crown shaping'. This operation involves reduction in the height and/or spread of the tree's canopy, where the tree is tending to outgrow its situation.

It must be stressed that crown reduction (like other pruning operations) must be carried out to growing points. 'Crown thinning', discussed above, should entail consideration of foliage to wood mass ratios.

The most undesirable extreme of a crown reduction operation, and one which is not carried out to growing points, is **lopping**. Not only are lopped trees severely disfigured but regrowth on such trees is generally dense, confined to too few growing points and weakly attached. As a result, regrowth from a lopped tree is difficult to manage effectively. Further, cuts on lopped trees are generally large, poorly placed, rarely callus effectively, and result in dieback, decay and, in many cases, the death of the tree.

Where a tree requires severe reduction or radical alteration to its aesthetically pleasing, natural growth habit, it is usually far better to consider replacing

a

b

Figure 25   **a** Sugar Gums (*Eucalyptus cladocalyx*) with weakly attached limbs, produced from a limited number of growing points following lopping.
b London Plane Trees (*Platanus × acerifolia*) that have been permanently disfigured by lopping.

the tree with a species more suitable for the situation, rather than mutilate the tree by lopping.

Storm-damaged trees may require reduction of damaged sections and shaping to assist framework development. Undamaged parts of the tree should not be pruned simply to give a 'balanced' appearance, as this will only stress the

Figure 26   Annual regrowth following pollarding of Crack Willow (*Salix fragilis*).

tree further. In time, the crown will re-establish naturally. Regrowth from damaged parts will require ongoing management, for example the selection of new leaders. In some cases, judicious thinning of undamaged parts, where these were previously protected, may help to minimise wind damage in the future.

A form of crown reduction known as **pollarding** is sometimes carried out on ornamental trees. This is a formal pruning practice *not* to be confused with lopping. Pollarding entails pruning back new growth, generally on an annual basis, to near previous pruning cuts. After a number of years, this results in the formation of large knobs of wound wood growth.

Pollarding may be carried out to contain tree size or to give a formal appearance. It does not allow a tree to develop its natural shape, and it can also result in dense growth causing severe shading. It has been observed that the severity of leaf scorch of plane trees (*Platanus* spp.) in some districts is less in pollarded

trees. A reason for this could be that the causal agent, the fungus *Gnomonia platani*, is better able to overwinter on infected wood in trees that have not been pollarded.

Few trees withstand pollarding, but examples of species that generally do are the Oriental Plane Tree (*Platanus orientalis*), London Plane Tree (*Platanus × acerifolia*), and the lindens (*Tilia* spp.)

Crown lifting

Crown lifting is the pruning operation to raise the crown or raise the canopy. It involves pruning or removal of branches to increase the distance between the base of the canopy and ground level. Normally crown lifting is carried out to improve access or provide visibility, and to remove obstruction beneath the canopy, particularly in the case of street trees.

This type of pruning should be carried out, if possible, before a tree

a   b

Figure 27   Crown lifting. **a** Before and **b** after lifting.

reaches maturity in order to avoid un-
necessarily large wounds and, to direct
growth into the most appropriate growing points. Refer to 'Formative pruning'
under 'Tree planting and establishment'
for further information.

Crown renewal

Crown renewal involves restoration of
the crown in the case of trees previously
lopped or otherwise severely damaged.
However, where lopped trees contain extensive decay and regrowth is poorly
attached, tree replacement *must* be considered. In situations where crown renewal
is considered, the process of corrective
pruning may take several years to complete. This procedure usually includes the
selection of leaders and sound scaffold
limbs, and crown thinning.

Wounds

The treatment of wounds, other than those caused by pruning, is addressed below. Although these wounds are generally referred to as 'bark wounds', damage is usually not confined to the bark only but sapwood may also be injured.

Basal wounds to the trunk are potentially more serious than wounds on the branches, because they are usually large in relation to the size of the trunk and resultant decay can affect the stability of the tree.

Causes of wounds

Wounds are commonly caused by:

- storms and lightning;
- motor vehicles such as cars, trucks and tractors;
- mowers and brush cutters; and
- vandals.

Treatment of wounds
'Bark wound' treatment

Treatment of wounds should be carried out by trimming damaged bark back to healthy tissue around the wound, avoiding unnecessary enlargement. Tools normally used for this purpose include chisels, gouges, a hammer and a sharp knife. The final cut to the bark edge should be made at a 90 degree angle to the sapwood. If present, areas of undamaged bark projecting into the wound should be retained to protect the sapwood below. Such projections do not hinder wound closure. All wound margins should be rounded as sharp points

Figure 28 Wounding of a tree butt caused by misuse of mowing machinery. Such a wound can be an entry point for wood-rotting organisms.

a

b

c

d

Figure 29 Treatment of a 'bark wound'.
a and **b** Trimming the damaged bark back to healthy tissue. **c** Smoothing the damaged wood within the wound. **d** The treated wound.

have been found to result in cambial die-back and the formation of cracks. Damaged wood within the wound should also be smoothed with a chisel and/or gouge, but only to the minimum level that will allow wound wood to move freely over the area. It is now accepted that wounds, like pruning cuts, should not be painted.

Bridge grafting and inarching

Trees severely damaged by ring-barking or stem-girdling may normally only be saved by bridge grafting. This entails trimming back torn bark, then bridging the wound by making a number of grafts across it. The grafts are generally made at intervals of 50–75 mm using short lengths of healthy shoot material. These

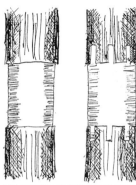

a

The wound to be bridge grafted must be specially trimmed to enable insertion of scion wood.

Each scion is trimmed with slanting cuts, top and bottom, to enable insertion into the trimmed wood.

The completed bridge graft should be well sealed in grafting wax.

b

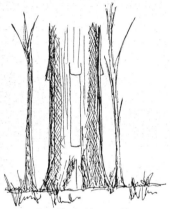

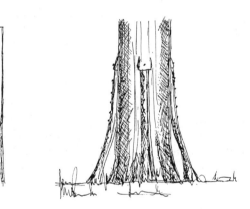

A number of bark strips must be removed from around the base of the tree to be inarched; a small flap of bark should be left at the top of each.

The tops of young seedlings planted about the tree base should be trimmed to enable insertion in the treated tree base.

The completed inarching should be well sealed in grafting wax.

Figure 30   **a** Bridge grafting and **b** inarching.

are each prepared with sloping cuts at either end (to facilitate cambial contact), and then inserted into slots cut in the bark. Each graft is secured and sealed in grafting wax.

Trees that have lost part of their root systems, due to mechanical injury, could have this replaced by inarching a young plant or plants of the same species or a compatible rootstock. These young plants are placed in the soil adjacent to the damaged tree and grafted into the trunk to replace the damaged root system. The plants are spaced at intervals of approximately 150 mm around the base of the tree if the damage is extensive.

Prevention of wounds

It is possible to prevent wounds caused by motor vehicles, works on construction sites and vandalism by erecting suitable barriers. Wounds caused by mowers and brush cutters may be prevented by applying selected herbicides around tree trunks, thereby eliminating the need to take this equipment close to trees. The chapter 'Tree planting and establishment', may be referred to for further details of staking and tree protection.

Maintaining tree health

I n a natural forest situation, trees exist in balance with their environment. Tree numbers and types are influenced by soil types, topography and climatic conditions. A natural cycle occurs in which elements taken up by the tree are returned to the soil through falling leaves, bark, fruits, branches and eventually entire trees. Macro- and micro-organisms aid in the process of converting this organic matter as well as maintaining an open and friable soil with good aeration and drainage.

Trees in an urban environment rarely have ideal growing conditions. Generally, they must contend with a host of stress-inducing factors including pollution, changes to the soil, and injury by people and machinery. Young vigorous trees are better able to withstand stress factors than mature, established trees, which may be severely affected by minor changes to their environment.

In this chapter stress-inducing factors are discussed and, where possible, preventive measures are suggested.

Air pollution

Air pollution is a major community problem. Sources of air pollutants include motor vehicles, smelters, brickworks, petrochemical plants and other industrial complexes, as well as evaporation from chlorinated swimming pools.

Air pollutants reduce the amount of sunlight available to plants, making them more susceptible to pest and disease attack. Some pollutants are known

Figure 31 An established tree on a construction site, the trunk well protected, but the root system is liable to damage from soil compaction and contamination.

to be toxic to plants and these include sulphur dioxide, fluorides, ozone, peroxylacetal nitrate (PAN), chlorides, ethylene and sulphides.

Symptoms of air-pollutant damage vary according to the particular pollutant and the susceptibility of the species. Common symptoms include necrosis and chlorosis, as well as flecking and silvering of leaves. Unfortunately, there is little that the arborist can do to cure these problems. However, the widespread planting of trees and implementation of emission controls should improve the situation. Planting of species known to resist air pollution should be considered in areas where there is a particular problem.

a

Changes to the soil profile

Through ignorance, many building and landscape contractors and engineers responsible for road construction and maintenance have killed trees by changing the soil profile. This is often due to mounding of soil around the trunks of mature trees during construction and maintenance of roads and roadside landscape 'improvement'. Such works also put the tree under stress through soil compaction, reduced soil aeration, alteration of natural drainage patterns and mechanical damage to root systems.

Another common cause of tree decline and death is the construction of buildings. Excavation of the site and installation of concrete slabs cause the severance of roots and alteration to soil aeration and drainage patterns. Loss of topsoil caused by such works is also a major problem, as this results in the removal of valuable nutrient reserves and organic matter. When undertaking such works, it is advisable to remove and stockpile the topsoil so that it can be replaced upon completion.

b

Figure 32   **a** Declining trees at the side of a road. These have soil raised and compacted about their butts; the result of road widening works.
b Declining trees in a car park, the result of soil compaction caused by motor vehicles. Remedial treatment including exclusion of traffic from some areas has been undertaken.

Soil compaction

Soil compaction is caused by vehicles and pedestrians, particularly when the soil is very wet or saturated. Vehicular traffic is the most common cause of compaction, however, pedestrian traffic over several years has been known to produce soil densities equivalent to concrete. Compaction results in soil particles being forced together, causing reduced water infiltration, poor drainage, restraining pressure against root growth, and impaired soil aeration. In turn, this leads to a smaller root system and thus stress on plants growing in affected areas. The management of traffic in vulnerable areas may be achieved by landscape design and planting strategies.

Compacted soils can be treated by

mechanical means such as coring, drilling, spiking or cultivation. These practices are best carried out when the soil is moist rather than wet or dry. However, when carrying out such procedures, one should be careful not to damage unduly the root system of plants.

Poor drainage

Poor drainage is generally the result of soil compaction, alteration of natural drainage patterns, or the presence of impermeable soils.

Alteration of natural drainage patterns is normally caused by changes in the soil profile or the construction of barriers such as buildings or retaining walls. Prevention of these problems is possible by incorporating adequate surface and/or subsurface drainage in works designs.

Impermeable soils are a common cause of poor drainage and these are often difficult to treat. Depending on the situation, shattering of the subsoil by deep ripping and the application of gypsum to flocculate certain clays may sometimes be the means of overcoming these problems.

Gas leakage

Leakage from underground gas lines is occasionally a cause of injury or death of trees. Leaking natural gas, although not toxic in itself, damages the tree by lowering the levels of oxygen in the soil. Symptoms of this disorder are similar to those of waterlogging. Often leaves on affected trees become cupped and scorched, and wilting may also occur. However, wilting is not normally as severe on gas-affected trees as it is on drought-stressed ones. Premature defoliation and dieback can also result. Severely gassed trees often die, although it normally takes gas leakage over more than one season for this to occur. Manufactured gas (coal gas) contains many substances which are toxic to plants, including carbon monoxide and

Figure 33 Declining tree in a new estate. Building of homes has caused a change in natural drainage patterns and soil profile. Tree roots have also been cut during the project.

hydrogen cyanide. Symptoms of poisoning include wilting and browning of leaves followed by branch dieback.

Treatment of a gas-affected site should begin with repair of the gas leak by the supply authority. Once the leak has been repaired the soil may be vented, but venting of heavy soils is generally ineffective. In the case of manufactured gas, the application of large amounts of water may assist in leaching out water-soluble toxins. It often takes longer than 12 months for gassed soil to return to an unaffected state. Replanting should not be carried out before this time. The local supply authority has equipment to test soils for the presence of gas.

Competition from neighbouring plants

Competition for water, growth elements and light is a very common cause of poor growth and development in trees. Prevention is the best solution to this problem, which may be overcome by ffective weed control, pruning of neighbouring plants and/or complete removal of plants considered of lesser value.

Figure 34　Closely planted trees competing with one another for light and nutrients. Note the poor growth habits.

Some plants can produce toxic substances from their roots, bark or leaves which inhibit or retard the growth of nearby plants, for example Black Walnut (*Juglans nigra*), River Red Gum (*Eucalyptus camaldulensis*), Couch (*Cynodon dactylon*) and fescues (*Festuca* spp.). This phenomenon is known as allelopathy.

Drought stress

The climate and available water should influence the choice of trees for planting.

During the summer months, especially when trees are young or growing in containers, a suitable irrigation program is an essential part of tree maintenance. Unfortunately, some people plant numerous trees in the winter but pay little attention to providing adequate watering for them during the summer months. This practice is both detrimental to tree survival and costly in terms of wasted resources.

Symptoms of lack of water include wilting, lack of vigour, loss of leaf colour and eventually terminal dieback.

Irrigation requirements are influenced by many factors including soil type, plant species, weather conditions, and whether the tree is growing in the ground or in a container. Deep watering is preferable to shallow watering as the latter can lead to undesirable shallow rooting. A tree's requirement for additional irrigation will be lessened if it is mulched.

Weather damage

Strong winds, frosts, heavy snowfalls and lightning sometimes result in damage to trees. Damage caused by strong winds and heavy snowfalls generally consists of broken limbs, but, in the case of lightning, the damage may also include splitting and burning of the bark. Frost damage usually results in burnt foliage but it can include death of shoots. Therefore, local weather conditions should be considered when selecting trees for planting.

Bracing, cleaning out or crown thinning may reduce the weight and leverage on limbs and lessen the damage caused by heavy snowfalls and strong winds.

Trees that have been severely damaged should be assessed to establish if remedial work, such as pruning and bracing, is warranted, or whether the tree should be removed.

Fire damage

Fire is a major cause of damage to trees in Australia, and other fire-prone areas of the world. Measures such as fuel reduction and planting of fire retardant species can prevent or reduce fire damage.

Where trees have been damaged by fire, remedial pruning is often required, while dead or severely damaged trees should be removed. However, in determining the remedial treatment required, one should not be too hasty; it is often wise to allow some time for possible regrowth to occur before carrying out pruning or tree removal. This applies particularly to species which have evolved in fire-prone areas, such as eucalypts (*Eucalyptus* spp.) and Coast Redwood (*Sequoia sempervirens*) which survive by producing new shoots from latent buds.

Figure 35   Sugar Gums (*Eucalyptus cladocalyx*) recovering from fire damage.

Nutritional disorders

A fertile soil is necessary for healthy plant growth. Such a soil has the chemical and physical properties that make growth elements available to plants. These properties are the presence of essential elements and organic matter, freedom from excessive soil salts, and a suitable acidity or alkalinity.

Where soils are not fertile, trees do not make sound growth. These unhealthy plants are more susceptible to disease than healthy trees and also less able to produce compounds such as gums, phenols and resins that combat pest attack. Signs of nutritional problems include poor growth and leaf symptoms.

Essential elements

Plants use water and certain elements from the soil together with carbon dioxide from the air, in the formation of plant tissues.

Using the energy of sunlight and the green pigment chlorophyll, plants are able to manufacture complex organic substances from the simple raw materials found in the soil and air. This process is called **photosynthesis** whereby water and atmospheric carbon dioxide are combined to form the carbohydrates (sugars and starches), which the plant uses as food to provide the energy necessary for its growth.

Some of the carbohydrates then combine with nitrogen and other elements absorbed by the roots to form proteins, which are the building blocks of all living cells. Only plants are able to manufacture carbohydrates and proteins from the simple compounds supplied by earth, air and water. As these organic compounds in turn serve as the basic foods for the animal world, the plant kingdom is the basis of all higher forms of life on earth.

While water and air supply the plant with hydrogen, carbon and oxygen, it is from the soil that the plant obtains the remaining thirteen elements essential for its growth. Six of the elements, namely nitrogen, potassium, phosphorus, calcium, magnesium and sulphur are required in larger amounts and form the bulk of the inorganic (non-carbon) portion of the plant. These elements are known as **major elements**. Of equal importance are the remaining elements (iron, zinc, chlorine, copper, manganese, boron and molybdenum) which are required in minute amounts only and so are often called **trace elements**. Their function is mainly to serve as activators (catalysts) for the complex chemical reactions taking place in the cells of all plants. In summary, elements required by plants for the performance of various functions are listed below with their chemical symbols.

Major elements of macronutrients

Carbon	C
Oxygen	O
Hydrogen	H
Nitrogen	N
Phosphorus	P
Potassium	K
Calcium	Ca
Magnesium	Mg
Sulphur	S

Trace elements or micronutrients

Manganese	Mn
Copper	Cu
Zinc	Zn
Molybdenum	Mo
Boron	B
Chlorine	Cl
Iron	Fe

The term a 'balanced diet' is widely used to describe an essential condition in the proper feeding of livestock and of human beings. For plants too, a balance between the growth elements present in the soil is necessary for optimum growth.

While earlier research workers were concerned with the action of each separate element on plant growth, the modern view emphasises also the importance of a balance between them for healthy plant growth. Excess of any one element may limit the uptake of another and so create a deficiency in the plant. Also if any one element is deficient in the soil, then growth will be limited despite a plentiful supply of all the others. Further, excessive amounts of elements required by the plant only in traces, such as boron, manganese, copper etc., are likely to prove toxic to growth.

If necessary, laboratory tests, such as tissue analysis and soil testing, can be used to determine the nutritional status of plants and/or soils.

Soil acidity and alkalinity

Many plants are affected by the degree of acidity or alkalinity of the soil. The pH value is a mathematical method of measuring acidity or alkalinity of a substance. Some plants can grow over a wide pH range, whereas some are sensitive to acidity and others are sensitive to alkalinity.

We may describe the acidity or alkalinity of soils, in terms of pH value, as follows.

Soil reaction	pH range
Strongly acid	4.0 to 5.4
Medium acid	5.5 to 5.9
Slightly acid	6.0 to 6.4
Very slightly acid	6.5 to 6.9
Neutral	7.0
Very slightly alkaline	7.1 to 7.5
Slightly alkaline	7.6 to 8.0
Medium alkaline	8.1 to 8.5
Strongly alkaline	8.6 to 10.0

In the case of soils, pHs below 4.0 or above 10.0 rarely exist. As the pH scale is logarithmic, each division is ten times more or less acid than its neighbour.

pH 6 is 10 times more acid than pH 7

pH 5 is 100 times more acid than pH 7

The availability of many essential elements required by plants can be affected by the pH range of the soil.

A slightly acid to neutral pH range of pH 6.5 to 7.0 is generally considered to be the best pH range for most plants to grow in.

The only time an arborist may need to influence soil pH is in a landscape project where soils or growing media are

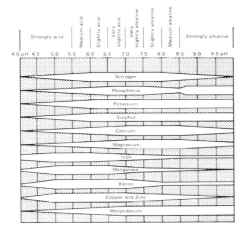

The availability to plants of nutrient elements varies with soil pH. Maximum availability is indicated by the widest part of the bar.

imported prior to planting. The appropriate soil pH value for the plant chosen should then be specified. In many other situations it is not practical to alter the soil pH, so plants should be selected on the basis of those which have evolved in a similar soil.

Testing of soil acidity may be carried out by using recognised electrometric or colormetric kits.

Fertilisers and their application

The importance of organic matter is often overlooked, but it is necessary to enhance the retention of nutrients and water and improve the soil structure. Suitable organic and/or artificial fertilisers can be used to supply or supplement growth elements. Organic matter can be provided by adding materials such as aged mature compost or leaf mould to the soil.

A fertiliser program may need to be part of a tree management program, particularly where fallen leaves and grass clippings from beneath a tree are not returned to the soil. Slow release and organic fertilisers may be applied at any time of the year. If applied in mid to late winter, these will be available to plants as growth commences. Soluble fertilis-

ers, which are readily available but are also easily leached from the soil, should only be applied when plants are actively growing. Fertilisers with a high nitrogen analysis should not be applied late in the growing season as this may force succulent growth which can be damaged by cold temperatures in autumn and winter. This can be particularly damaging when fertilisers are applied as foliar sprays.

It is usual to apply complete fertilisers containing nitrogen, phosphorus and potassium plus trace elements. However, the required levels of such elements will depend on the situation and the plants grown, for instance some members of the family Proteaceae, such as certain *Banksia*, *Protea* and *Grevillea* species are intolerant of high levels of phosphorus.

Methods of fertiliser application include surface application, soil incorporation, foliar spraying and trunk injection.

• *Soil incorporation* is the most common method of fertilising large ornamental trees. The soil may be spiked, drilled or cored and solid fertiliser broadcast, then watered in. A hand or power auger may be used to drill holes in the soil, before placing a mixture of fertiliser and soil or organic matter in each hole. These procedures ensure that fertilisers are placed where they are wanted, in the soil near the tree's roots. In the case of trees with spreading crowns, the feeding root zone is normally considered to be from about half the radius from the trunk to the dripline, and about an equivalent distance beyond the dripline.

For trees with a fastigiate habit, the feeding root zone will be beyond the dripline of the tree; a distance between half the height and the full height of the tree would not be unreasonable. The actual extent and depth of the tree's root system will be dependent on many factors which include species characteristics, soil type, soil profile, availability of moisture and nutrients, and competition from other plants. In spite

of all these considerations, it is undesirable to carry out these procedures
close to the tree trunk.

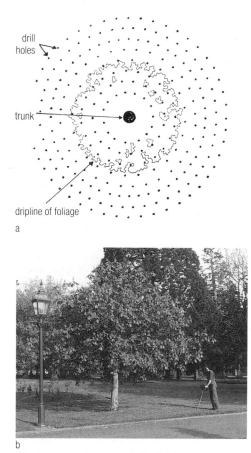

a

b

Figure 36   a and **b** Soil incorporation. A method of
applying solid fertilisers to amenity trees.

- *Foliar spraying* of fertiliser entails the
  application of suitable water-soluble
  fertilisers over the tree's foliage. This
  is not a common method of fertilising
  mature trees but it is often carried out
  on young trees, together with the
  application of solid fertilisers to the
  soil. Fertilisers applied as foliar sprays
  do not run the risk of being locked up
  or leached in certain soils. Further,

suitable soluble fertilisers applied in
this fashion are rapidly absorbed
through the leaves and assimilated by
the plant. For these reasons, foliar
spraying is often regarded as a most
suitable method of correcting deficien-
cies of certain micro-elements in plants.
- *Trunk injection* is also a means of direct
  fertilising; however, the authors consider that it should be used only as a
  last resort as making holes in the trunk
  exposes it to the danger of cambial dieback and the entry of pathogens. Where
  access to the root system is limited and
  foliar application is impractical, then
  trunk injection may be the only alternative. It should be realised, however,
  that this method cannot be used as fre-
  quently as soil incorporation or foliar
  spraying because it causes damage.

Soil salinity

Salting inhibits the uptake of water by
plants and causes changes to the soil
structure. This can result in reduced po-
rosity, and therefore reduced infiltration, and increased surface runoff.

Excessive levels of salts in the soil are
toxic to plants. The increase in salt levels
may be brought about by a rise in the
watertable bringing salt from lower levels up into the root zone, or by excessive
application of fertilisers. A rise in the
watertable may be due to reduced tree
cover, irrigation, or alteration of natural
drainage patterns.

Saline soils can be treated by improving irrigation and drainage practices to
lower the watertable and leach soil salts.
Tree planting is also an important factor
in salinity control as it lowers the watertable by decreasing runoff and increasing evapo-transpiration. Improvements
may be evident in as little as three or
four years after planting.

Soil salinity may be determined by
use of a conductivity meter.

Weeds,
pests and diseases

The control of weeds, pests and diseases is an important aspect of tree care. In addition to the information set out below, specialised texts that deal with this subject are listed under the 'Pests, diseases, weeds and their control' section of 'References and further reading'.

Weeds

The control of weed growth, particularly around young trees, is most important. Weeds compete with other plants for soil moisture and nutrients. They also harbour pests and diseases as well as looking unsightly. It is also known that toxins produced by certain plants can inhibit the growth of others; this phenomenon is known as **allelopathy**.

Weeds can be classified into two main groups — annuals and perennials.

Annual weeds

Annual weeds complete their life cycle in one growing season. Examples of this group include Winter Grass (*Poa annua*), Chickweed (*Stellaria media*), and Sow Thistle (*Sonchus oleraceus*).

Control of these weeds is best undertaken before flowering, as dictated by the old saying, 'one year seeding — ten years weeding'.

Various *mulches* such as straw and shredded bark may be applied to suppress annual weed growth. These also conserve soil moisture and influence soil temperatures.

Mechanical means of control, such as chip hoeing, may also be used to control annual weeds. Such methods rely upon burying the weeds or decapitating them. Generally, these measures are more effective if carried out on hot, dry days. Continual disturbance of the soil causes a depletion of organic matter and damage to the structure. New weed seed populations are brought closer to the soil surface (in a more favourable position for germination) by routine cultivation. Deep cultivation can also cause damage to the roots of desirable plants, and so should be avoided.

Chemical control of annual weeds is also possible, though the cost of chemicals is often high when compared with mechanical means. However, application on a large scale often requires less labour than mechanical control measures, and, depending on the choice of herbicide, should cause less damage to the soil structure.

In clean-soil situations, the emergence of weeds can be prevented by application of certain **soil-active herbicides**, generally referred to as 'pre-emergent herbicides'. These are absorbed by seed, germinating seeds and sometimes very young seedlings, killing them before they can become established. The amount of organic matter in a soil, the solubility of the herbicide and the soil type will all influence how deeply the herbicide will leach into the soil. These properties will also affect the selectivity of the herbicide. For instance, a tree growing in a light sandy soil may be killed by a certain soil-active herbicide,

41

whereas the same tree in a heavy clay soil may not be damaged as the herbicide is not able to leach down to the root system.

The higher the rate of application, the longer a soil-active herbicide is likely to persist in the soil. Some chemicals, when applied at recommended rates for pre-emergent weed control, may persist for up to six weeks. Whereas, at higher rates, these same chemicals can act as sterilants and persist for more than 12 months. Certain soil-active herbicides used for pre-emergent weed control in arboriculture include simazine and oxadiazon.

Usually, post-emergent chemical control of annual weeds can also be carried out, by using **contact herbicides**. When these chemicals are sprayed onto weeds, they will desiccate the parts with which they come into contact. Examples of such herbicides include paraquat and diquat.

Perennial and biennial weeds

These weeds live for more than one growing season; biennials complete their life cycle over two growing seasons, and perennials live for three or more growing seasons. For the purposes of weed control, both groups are generally treated in the same way. Examples of perennial weeds include Couch (*Cynodon dactylon*), sedges (*Cyperus* spp.), docks and sorrels (*Rumex* spp.).

Unlike annual weeds, perennial weeds generally produce a deep root system from which they have the capacity to regenerate. For this reason, infrequent cultivation is usually ineffective in controlling them. Effective mechanical control entails complete plant removal prior to seeding.

The use of herbicides should be seriously considered for the control of these weeds. In clean-soil situations, certain soil-active herbicides may be used to prevent emergence, the choice of which will depend upon the herbicide's selectivity and spectrum of control.

Post-emergent control of perennial weeds is best carried out by using foliar-applied **translocated herbicides**. Though slower in action than contact herbicides, these chemicals are absorbed through the leaves, circulated throughout the plant including the root system, thus killing the whole plant. For best results, translocated herbicides should be applied during periods of active plant growth. Rates of application should be adhered to, as excessive rates may cause translocated herbicides to act as contact herbicides, thereby rendering them less effective. Glyphosate is a commonly used, foliar applied, translocated (non soil-residual) herbicide.

Pests

Pests that from time-to-time cause damage to plants include insects, allied forms and vertebrate pests.

Insects and allied forms

Insects and allied forms such as mites, normally cause most pest damage to plants. Adult insects are characterised by having three main body segments, three pairs of legs, antennae and, in many cases, wings. Adult mites, however, have two main body segments and four pairs of legs; mites are often not visible to the unaided eye. A characteristic of insects and allied forms is that they are capable of rapid multiplication. Details of the damage caused by these pests are given in the following tables.

Many piercing and sucking pests are vectors of virus diseases, since they transfer infected sap from one plant to another.

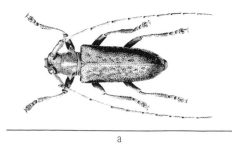

a

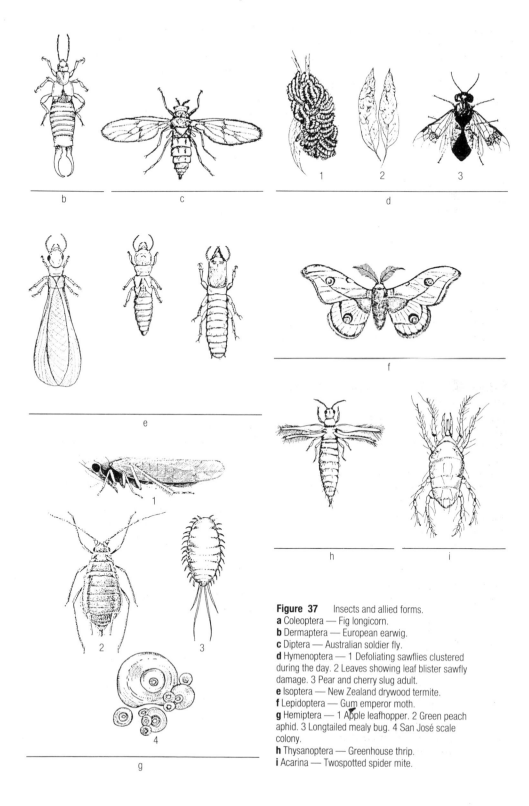

Figure 37 Insects and allied forms.
a Coleoptera — Fig longicorn.
b Dermaptera — European earwig.
c Diptera — Australian soldier fly.
d Hymenoptera — 1 Defoliating sawflies clustered during the day. 2 Leaves showing leaf blister sawfly damage. 3 Pear and cherry slug adult.
e Isoptera — New Zealand drywood termite.
f Lepidoptera — Gum emperor moth.
g Hemiptera — 1 Apple leafhopper. 2 Green peach aphid. 3 Longtailed mealy bug. 4 San José scale colony.
h Thysanoptera — Greenhouse thrip.
i Acarina — Twospotted spider mite.

Table 2   Chewing damage caused by some insect pests of ornamental trees

Pest	Stage of life cycle	Plant parts affected	Symptoms of damage
Coleoptera beetles weevils (borers)	adult or larva (grub)	leaves, flowers, buds, fruit	chewing of leaves, buds, flowers and fruit
Dermaptera earwigs	adult and nymph	leaves, buds, flowers, fruit, roots	chewing of leaves, buds, flowers, fruit and roots
Diptera flies	larva (grub or maggot)	leaves, fruit, seed	tunnelling, mining or skeletonising of leaves tunnelling and chewing of fruit and seed
Hymenoptera sawflies wasps	larva (spitfire or slug)	leaves	blistering, mining, skeletonising and chewing of leaves
Lepidoptera moths butterflies	larva (leaf-miner, looper caterpillar)	leaves	chewing, mining, skeletonising and rolling of leaves
Phasmatodea stick insects	adult or nymph	leaves	chewing and loss of leaves

Table 3   Sucking damage* caused by some insect and mite pests of ornamental trees

Pest	Stage of life cycle	Plant parts affected	Symptoms of damage
Hemiptera bugs aphids leaf hoppers lerps/psyllids mealybugs scales whiteflies	adult or nymph	leaves flowers, fruit, stems, shoots	mottling, yellowing, wilting, distortion, death and loss of leaves marking, distortion, size reduction, and death of flowers, fruit, stems and shoots
Thysanoptera thrips *Acarina* mites		flowers, fruit, stems, shoots	marking, distortion, size reduction, and death of flowers, fruit, stems and shoots
	adult and nymph	leaves, shoots fruit	yellowing, blistering, rolling, silvering, webbing and witches' broom malformation of leaves and shoots malformation, russetting

* The presence of sucking insects is generally detected by the presence of excretions, particularly sugary 'honeydew'. Other insects, especially ants, are attracted by this excretion, and it can also host the growth of sooty mould fungus.

Table 4 Boring damage* caused by some insect pests of ornamental trees

Pest	Stage of life cycle	Plant parts affected	Symptoms of damage
Coleoptera beetles/weevils	larva (borer)	stem/trunk, bark, roots	tunnelling in wood and shelling of bark
Hymenoptera wasps	adults and larva	stem/trunk	eggs laid in tunnels by adults hatch and bore into wood
Isoptera termites/white ants	adult	stem/trunk, limbs	tunnelling within the plant and eventual collapse
Lepidoptera moths	larva (borer)	stem/trunk, shoots, fruit	tunnelling of trunk/stem, shoots and fruit

* Some boring pests are associated with the spread of certain fungal diseases.

Table 5 Gall formation damage caused by some insect pests of ornamental trees

Pest	Stage of life cycle	Plant parts affected	Symptoms of damage
Diptera flies	larva	leaves, stems	
Hemiptera aphids scale/psyllids	adult and nymph	stems, shoots, leaves	Initially these pests cause sucking or chewing damage and excretion of enzymes. The plant reacts to this damage with abnormal cell division which manifests itself as gall formation.
Hymenoptera wasps	larva	leaves, stems	
Thysanoptera thrips	adult and nymph	leaves	

Vertebrate pests

These pests of trees include certain birds, arborial mammals and rodents. Damage caused to trees by birds is normally confined to the fruit, but some birds also attack other plant parts, for instance, cockatoos will dig into trees in search of grubs and even ring-bark limbs. The possum is an example of an arborial mammal responsible for harming ornamental trees. These creatures wound the bark and chew leaves and fruit, and may even cause death of the tree by continual defoliation. Other mammals that damage trees include rodents, such as rabbits and hares, which usually cause problems by chewing on young trees. Kangaroos and feral goats may also harm young trees.

Monitoring of pest populations and their activities should be part of any pest management program as this will determine firstly, whether the damage caused warrants control and, secondly, it will monitor the effectiveness of the program. Lure jars and pheromone traps are two common means of achieving this. Control measures are described below.

Control measures

- *Quarantine measures* that stop the introduction of undesirable pests are an effective means of preventing pest damage. However, quarantine is ineffective when a pest, whether native or introduced, is present.
- *Cultural techniques* that enable a tree to grow in a vigorous condition are the most desirable pest control techniques, since stressed trees are more prone to attack by some pests than healthy trees. The use of pest-resistant or immune varieties can also be of value in preventing pest attack, an example being the propagation of Northern Spy and some Malling Merton apple rootstocks for woolly aphid resistance.
- *Hygienic practices* that involve the elimination and destruction of pest-infested plant material are also important control measures and these include pruning out and burning infested wood.
- *Biological control* is an important pest management technique which can be integrated with direct pest control methods such as the use of pesticides. An example of biological pest control is the conservation of predatory ladybirds (*Stethorus* spp.), the larvae of which feed on certain 'sucking' plant pests. Another example is the parasitic wasp *Aphelinus mali* which oviposits its eggs into the body of a Woolly Aphid (*Eriosoma lanigerum*), thereby killing it. Other notable biological control agents include certain mites and viral, fungal or bacterial diseases. An example is the bacterial insecticide *Bacillus thuringiensis* which is widely available commercially, and may be applied as a spray for control of lepidopterous larvae.

Although often underestimated, birds such as silvereyes (*Zosterops* spp.) and honeyeaters (*Meliphaga* spp.) are also important pest control agents. These can be attracted to the garden by planting suitable flowering and fruiting species as well as plants that provide protection or nesting sites.
- *Direct control of pests by non-chemical means* is also possible although such techniques are mainly confined to commercial horticulture. An example of a non-chemical control specific to arboriculture is the installation of metal skirts around the trunks of selected specimen trees to prevent possum attack.
- *Chemicals* may also be used directly for controlling pests; however, careless selection and use of pesticides should be avoided. This method of pest control may be unwarranted if the damage caused by the pest is minimal but, where trees are in danger of being defoliated for the second consecutive season, chemical control is usually desirable. Chemicals selected for controlling pests should pose the lowest possible threat to the environment, the operator and any biological control agents that may be present. In many instances the spraying of pesticides on large ornamental trees is simply not practical for reasons of safety and efficiency. The types of pesticides used should be alternated to reduce the possibility of resistant populations developing.

Leaf-chewing pests, such as caterpillars, may be treated with **stomach poisons** that are applied to and adhere to the surface of the leaf. Carbaryl is an example of a stomach poison.

Insects that suck sap, mine or chew the leaves of plants may be controlled with **systemic pesticides** which are usually applied through the foliage. These chemicals disseminate throughout the plant. It is also possible to obtain systemic pesticides that are soil-applied and translocate upwards from the roots. Although the use of soil-applied upward-translocating pesticides is not uncommon in amenity horticulture, their use in arboriculture has been minimal. The authors believe that more research in this area is warranted. Examples of systemic insecticides include dimethoate and diazinon. Some systemic pesticides may also be trunk injected but, as indicated previously, the authors believe that making unnecessary holes in a trunk should be avoided.

It is also possible to control some pests with **contact pesticides**. These normally enter the pest through the cuticle or respiratory system and kill by disrupting vital areas such as the nervous or respiratory systems. Pesticides with contact action include pyrethrins and white oil. Fumigant type pesticides, such as maldison, are also regarded as being contact in action.

Pests such as borers can only be controlled with systemic chemicals when they inhabit the active conductive tissues of the plant. Where these pests are a problem in non-conductive heartwood, systemic pesticides are ineffective.

In situations where galls have been caused by the presence of insects, it is too late to control the problem. Control of the next generation is only possible at this stage, and this is generally unwarranted.

Diseases
Causes of disease

- *Fungi* are the most common causes of infectious plant diseases. They are simple plants that are devoid of chlorophyll, and they generally consist of a body or mycelium composed of fine filaments known as 'hyphae'. These fungal bodies also produce minute spores for the purpose of reproduction. Fungi are classified according

a

b

Figure 38 **a** An established European Beech (*Fagus sylvatica*) declining due to fungal disease attack.
b Detail of the fungal growth on the base of the trunk.

to their structure and the types of spores produced.

- *Bacteria* are simple, microscopic single-celled plants that contain no chlorophyll and are capable of multiplication by cell division.
- *Virus and virus-like diseases* are caused by agents found in living host cells. These agents are composed of genetic material and proteins, and can only be seen with the aid of an electron microscope. Classic symptoms of virus diseases are irregular mosaic blotches on the leaves; yellowing of leaf margins, tips or interveinal areas; and yellow line patterns. Other symptoms associated with certain virus diseases include streaking of flowers, excessive branching, foliar ring spots, leaf rolling, and various malformations.
- *Nematodes* are microscopic, non-segmented roundworms. Most plant parasitic nematodes invade root cells causing damage and dysfunction of the vascular system. Some are involved in the transmission of viral and fungal diseases of plants by secreting saliva into the plant while feeding.
- *Parasitic flowering plants* include the true mistletoes which are often seen growing on limbs of trees on which they depend for water and minerals.

Symptoms of disease

The presence of many infectious plant diseases may be detected by the appearance of symptoms manifested in the host plants. These symptoms include:

- blights
- rots
- wilts
- mildews
- rusts
- smuts
- spots
- leaf curl
- galls
- cankers and scabs and
- mosaics and yellows.

Although certain symptoms are classic indicators of particular plant diseases, others can cause confusion. For this reason, the diagnosis of many plant diseases is often best left to recognised institutions, such as government agriculture departments and plant research laboratories, who will generally offer advice on disease control.

Control measures

- Like pests, diseases can be prevented and controlled by *quarantine measures*.
- *Cultural techniques*, such as the use of resistant or immune varieties, and other techniques including cleaning out, crown thinning and the correct placement and execution of pruning cuts, are also valuable disease control measures. The level of control is increased by using hygienic practices such as the burning of infected plant parts (leaves, prunings etc.). Pruning equipment should be sterilised immediately after using it on infected plants.
- An important aspect of disease control, which is often overlooked, is the *improvement of overall plant vigour* and growing conditions. A healthy plant will resist and defend itself against pathogens more effectively than a stressed plant that has less energy to spare for defence responses. Identification and correction of stress-inducing factors, such as water stress, soil compaction and other soil/root disorders, should be considered when assessing any disease problem.
- *Biological control* of plant diseases is also possible to a limited extent. For instance, control of the bacterial disease crown gall, (*Agrobacterium* spp.) is carried out by dipping roots, cuttings and seeds of susceptible species such as the Peach (*Prunus persica*) in suspensions of the antagonistic bacterium *Agrobacterium rhizogenes*.
- It is also possible to control some diseases directly by *physical methods* and an example of this is the pruning of mistletoes (parasitic flowering plants of several genera including *Amyema*, *Dendrophthoe* and *Notothixos*) from infested trees.

- *Chemical control* can be used for certain fungal and bacterial diseases. Products used include non-systemic **protectants** and systemic **eradicants**. Protectants are applied to leaf surfaces to protect a plant *before* disease infection occurs, whereas eradicants are applied *after* infection has occurred and are absorbed by the host plant for curative disease control.

Though it is possible to control some bacterial and fungal diseases by chemical means, the same cannot be said of virus and virus-like diseases. Curative treatment of virus diseases entails special laboratory practices including heat treatment and plant tissue culture.

Chemical control of nematodes may be carried out with chemicals having modes of action previously described under 'Pests'. The control of parasitic flowering plants by chemical means is also being investigated. Certain translocated herbicides have been used in trials at low dosages for this purpose.

Successful control of some diseases in amenity trees is not always possible. For trees with advanced infections of wood-rotting diseases there is no cure and trees that are dangerously unsafe due to such infections must be removed. The felling and burning of infected trees is an effective sanitation measure to prevent the spread of many fungal, bacterial and viral diseases.

Cavity treatment

Occasionally, cavities will develop from wounds in trunks and branches of trees. Small wounds on vigorous, healthy trees are likely to be compartmentalised and not develop into cavities. However, such wounds may later be invaded by pests and decay-causing organisms, particularly on trees of low vigour, and thus develop into cavities. Healthy trees normally have the ability to compartmentalise decay, thereby limiting its spread through the tree. Details of the compartmentalisation process are discussed under 'Tree growth and development'.

Any work that is done in the course of tree surgery, should not inhibit the tree's ability to compartmentalise decay. Recommended modern techniques, such as making final pruning cuts outside the branch bark ridge and branch collar, should be adhered to. It is now recognised that the draining of cavities and water pockets by drilling holes is not desirable as this practice will damage the compartmental walls, thus furthering decay. For this reason also, rod bracing of cavities cannot be recommended.

The treatment of cavities need not entail filling. It may be sufficient to remove only enough loose and badly decayed wood from inside the cavity to improve its appearance, but it is not uncommon for unfilled cavities in park trees to be filled with rubbish or have fires lit in them by vandals.

The aim of cavity filling is to protect the cavity from further damage, encourage wound closure and, in some instances, improve the tree's appearance.

Filling should begin with the removal of rubbish and loose wood. At this stage it should not be necessary to chisel and gouge out decayed wood.

Once initial cleaning out is completed, the cavity can be filled. For this purpose, not-toxic, flexible, water-resistant materials such as urethane foams are recommended. Urethane foam is sold as a two-part product that is mixed prior to filling and is available in a range of formulations and densities. Check the product for suitability. For best results, urethane foam should only be used in warm weather. Care should be taken when mixing, for some foams may release toxic fumes. Use protective equipment or clothing if required.

A covering material, such as heavy gauge plastic sheeting, can be stapled or tacked in place when the cavity is being filled and while the foam filler is setting. Once the filler has set (generally after 15 minutes) the sheeting can be removed and the foam neatly trimmed. In areas where vandals or animals are likely to interfere with the filler, a harder protective skin material, such as car body filler, may be applied over the foam filler. This can then be painted to make the filled cavity less obvious and more aesthetically pleasing. The use of concrete or bricks for filling cavities is not recommended; these materials are heavy and inflexible, do not provide support and can damage chainsaws when the tree is eventually removed.

In some situations, particularly in the case of very large cavities where the expense of a complete fill is not warranted,

a

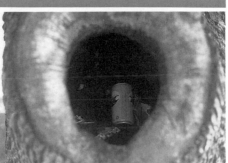

b

c

d

e

f

g

Figure 39   a and **b** Cavity in a tree in public park
being used as a rubbish bin.
c Rubbish and loose wood being removed.
d Cavity is covered with heavy duty plastic prior to
filling.
e Plastic sheeting trimmed with opening at the top for
pouring in the foam filling.
f Mixing of the two parts of the polyurethane foam filler.
g Pouring in the mixed foam materials prior to
expansion.

Figure 39   continued on page 52

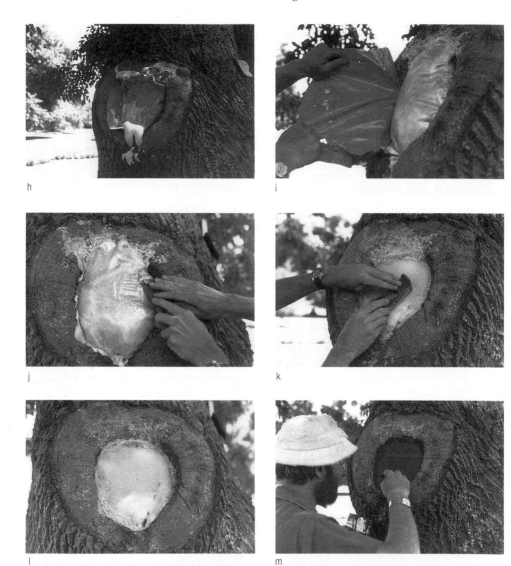

h

i

j

k

l

m

partial (basal) filling may be carried out to prevent build-up of water and debris in the base of the cavity.

It should be noted that cavity treatment does nothing to improve tree vigour, health, stability or strength.

Figure 39   *(continued)*
h Note the excess foam forced out from behind the plastic sheet.
i Plastic sheet is removed after the foam has set.
j and **k** Excess foam is trimmed to the edge of wound tissue and smoothed and flattened to provide a surface for wound tissue to grow over.
l Foam surface ready for application of hard surfacing material or paint.
m Painting to make the filled cavity less obvious and more aesthetically pleasing.

Bracing

It is not uncommon for some trees to develop weak and unsafe branch structures during the course of normal growth. These structures include co-dominant stems and heavy horizontal limbs. Many structural problems can be eliminated early in the tree's life by formative pruning. Details may be found under 'Pruning', 'Tree planting and establishment' and 'Tree growth and development'. However, in cases where young trees have an inherently poor branching habit, removal and replacement with more suitable specimens should be considered if corrective pruning to re-shape the tree has not been successful.

Mature trees that are structurally imperfect, but not considered to be dangerous, may be preserved by bracing. However, mature trees assessed as being too dangerous and unsound to brace should be removed without delay Trees considered to be valuable are worth the expenditure of time and effort necessary to preserve them. However, structurally imperfect, young specimens of common species are better removed, and the site replanted.

In many cases, trees judged to be safe have dropped limbs or collapsed under load or adverse conditions such as high winds, heavy fruiting, snow and extreme heat. Properly fitted braces undoubtedly improve the tree's chances of withstanding such forces.

Bracing is primarily a preventive measure. In practice, this means that a recognisable weakness, such as a co-dominant stem in a mature tree, should be treated *before* it begins to fracture. It is the responsibility of the arborist to inform the tree owner that *bracing cannot be guaranteed to provide total tree safety*. After considering the arborist's assessment of the situation, the final decision as to whether a tree will be braced or removed lies with the owner.

The treatment of co-dominant stems in mature trees by removal of one of the leaders is not recommended. Such 'treatment' usually results in an unaesthetic specimen which still has an inherent structural weakness. This would also constitute over-pruning, upsetting the balance between the static and dynamic mass of the plant.

In order to carry out cable and rod bracing it is necessary to drill holes in trees. Although drilling of holes is not generally a recommended practice in arboriculture, in the case of cable and rod bracing, these small wounds are preferable to larger wounds resulting from limb collapse.

Some species are not ideally suited to cable and rod bracing since they do not readily compartmentalise wounds, for example, *Brachychiton* spp., *Erythrina* spp., *Liriodendron* spp., *Populus* spp. and *Salix* spp.

All materials used in bracing should be galvanised or plated, or made of stainless steel, to prevent rusting. Although expensive, the use of stainless steel rods and eye bolts may be superior.

For reasons of safety, periodic checks of all bracing should be carried out, perhaps twice per year.

Cable bracing

Cable bracing is the most common form of bracing. It involves the placement of one or more flexible steel wire ropes between trunks and branches, or the trunk and a heavy horizontal limb, to prevent *excessive movement* and stress on crotches and branches.

The cable bracing procedure should begin with making a decision on the best position for the brace.

Co-dominant stems may be supported by positioning the cable between the stems, approximately two-thirds of their length up from the crotch or fork, as illustrated.

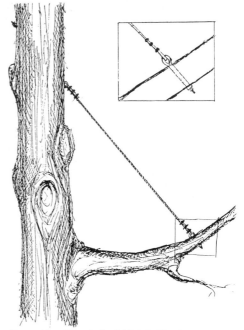

Figure 41 Heavy horizontal limb that has been cable braced.

Figure 40 Co-dominant stem that has been cable braced.

Multiple co-dominant stems should be treated by bracing the weaker stems to the stronger ones, in the manner already described. In some situations this may entail installing more than one cable in a particular stem. If this is required, only one cable should be secured to each point of attachment. On any leader, the cables should be installed at least 300 mm apart.

A heavy horizontal limb can be braced by positioning the cable between the trunk and the limb. The cable should be secured approximately two-thirds of the way along the limb at an angle of at least 45 degrees to the limb. As well as trying to achieve the correct angle of the cable, the operator should secure the brace as high as possible in sound wood that is strong enough to withstand the expected stresses.

In order to secure the cable brace, holes must be drilled in the trunk and/or limb for installation of threaded rod, eye-bolts or screw-eyes. Holes for threaded rod or eye-bolts should be the same diameter as the rod or bolt, but screw-eyes in soft-wooded species require a hole 3 mm less than the diameter of the screw. This can be reduced to 1.5 mm in hard-wooded species. Holes for screw-eyes must be slightly longer than the screw itself, which should always be fitted to full length with the eye hard up against the wood.

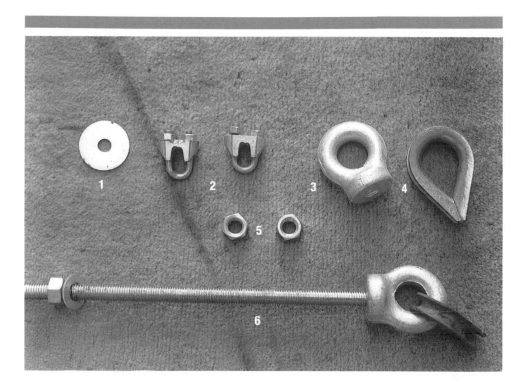

Figure 42   Cable bracing materials
1 large diameter washer
2 steel wire rope grips
3 eye-nut
4 thimble
5 nuts
6 eye-nut, thimble and threaded rod assembled and ready for use.

Holes should be drilled through or into the centre of the diameter of the branch or trunk and at an angle that will align them with the cable. A rope can be placed along the proposed cable route to assist in the alignment of the holes. Wherever possible, holes should not be located at or near branch unions or in areas of decayed wood. Hand or power augers can be used to drill the holes. Electric drills often require a portable generator as a power source and long extension leads to be carried up into the tree which can be a problem, especially in wet weather. It is possible to purchase cordless drills having sufficient power for most cabling work. Chainsaw drill

attachments and other lightweight two-stroke drills are also available and can be recommended for drilling large diameter holes or holes in large trunks. Generally threaded rod or eye-bolts are then installed. These are considered to be the strongest means of securing the brace, especially in soft wood or trees known to be poor compartmentalisers; screw-eyes should only be used in strong, sound timbers. In such timbers screw-eyes may be particularly useful when cabling a weak branch to a point on the trunk which would normally necessitate a larger wound (drill hole) than would be needed to provide adequate support. In such instances, using a screw-eye could be recommended as the least invasive and damaging method.

Eye-bolts and screw-eyes are selected for the job in hand, according to estimated loadings. Diameters of more than 12 mm are rarely needed. A guide to the selection of eye-bolts, threaded rods and steel wire rope is set out in Table 6 below.

Figure 43   **a** Drilling hole using Atom drilling attachment on chainsaw. Rope tied between the stems to assist in the alignment of the holes.
b, **c** and **d** Installing eye-bolt, tightening nut and cutting off excess thread.

e Securing an end of the cable brace with steel wire rope grips. Note the wire rope is passed around a thimble to protect the steel wire rope and the eye-bolt.
f Tensioning the cable brace with a hand winch.
g Completion of the cable brace.

Table 6 A guide to the selection of hardware for cable bracing

Diameter of limb	Diameter of eye-bolt or threaded rod	Diameter of galvanised steel wire rope
up to 150 mm	6–8 mm	4–6 mm
150 mm–300 mm	8–12 mm	6–8 mm
300 mm and larger	12–14 mm	8–10 mm

A nut and washer are required for securing any eye-bolt or threaded rod. The washer must be recessed or countersunk, but only to the cambium. This is done by neatly removing sufficient bark with a chisel or gouge before fitting the rod. In the past, washers of various shapes have been used for this purpose, but it is now usual to use a standard round washer and circular countersink. Wounds with pointed apices (such as those made to accommodate a diamond-shaped washer) are detrimental to sound callus development, as discussed in the chapter 'Wounds'.

Where an eye-bolt or threaded rod is installed at an angle through a branch or trunk, a piece of galvanised water pipe or aluminium tubing may be cut with one end at an angle to act as a spacer between the nut and washer. Eye-nuts with large collars should be counter-sunk.

Steel wire rope used in bracing consists of a number of strands grouped and layed together around a central core. Each strand is made up of a number of individual wires twisted together. The central core may be of wire or fibre impregnated with oil for lubrication and rust prevention. Round-strand fibre-core rope is used for cable bracing as it is more flexible and, therefore, easier to work with. Table 7 below gives specifications for this rope. Steel wire ropes of different construction used for other purposes will have different safe working load (SWL) specifications and safety factors.

When securing steel wire rope to an eye it must be passed around an appropriately sized thimble. This prevents the rope from rubbing on the eye, breaking the galvanising and weakening the rope. Threaded rod used in cable bracing is fitted with a suitably sized eye-nut to secure the steel wire rope.

Wire rope grips, sometimes known as wire bulldog grips, are normally used to seize steel wire rope around the thimble and eye-nut. The wire rope grips are secured approximately six rope diameters apart, with saddles and lock nuts facing the standing or load-bearing part of the rope as illustrated. Wire rope grips should be tightened in sequence starting with the one closest to the eye. The nuts on each grip are tightened a little at a time until there is good compression of the

Table 7 Specifications for galvanised general purpose steel wire rope, round-strand, 6 × 19, fibre-core (based on information contained in Australian Wire Industries Pty Ltd, Waratah Wire Rope General Information)

Nominal diameter tolerance	Breaking load strain**		Average mass kg/100 m	Safe working load*** (SWL)	
	tonnes force	kilonewton		tonnes force	kilonewton
6 mm*	1.79	17.6	12.4	0.6	5.8
8 mm	3.15	30.9	22.1	1.0	10.3
10 mm	4.9	48.2	34.6	1.6	16.0
12 mm	7.09	69.5	49.8	2.4	23.2

* diameter tolerance +6%–1% for ropes up to 7 mm
** minimum breaking force at 1570 MPa (megapascal)
*** safe working load based upon a safety factor of 3 as recommended for static guy ropes

wires, and without breaking the galvanising on the rope. Australian standards
recommend that three wire rope grips be
used for securing each end of the rope.

Short cable runs can be tensioned by
securing the rope at both ends, leaving
sufficient length of eye-bolt or threaded
rod protruding from one or both auger
holes, and then drawing up the rope by
tightening the nut on the eye-bolt or
threaded rod. Considerable experience
is needed to achieve correct tension by
this method, as the eye of each bolt
should finish hard up against the branch
or trunk. If the shanks of eye-bolts are
left protruding, they may bend or be
weakened under heavy load; this may
also cause the eye-bolt to damage the
drill hole if pulled off centre.

A more accurate method of tensioning, particularly on long cable runs, is to
fit both eye-bolts or threaded rods and
secure the cable at one end only. Tension is then placed on the wire rope by
drawing it through the other eye with a
small handwinch. When correct tension
is gained the steel wire rope can then be
seized and the excess cut off. *Cable braces
should not be over tensioned.* Correct
tension should minimise 'snatching' in
gusty winds without placing unnatural
stress on trunks or branches. Remember
that bracing should be preventive not
supportive, so cables should be 'snug'
rather than tight.

Rope ends should be cut cleanly with
wire rope cutting pliers, leaving approximately 25 mm protruding from the last
grip.

Rod bracing

Rod bracing is a less common form of
bracing. It entails placing steel rod (generally threaded) in the trunk of a multi-
stemmed tree. This form of bracing is
normally used in conjunction with cable
bracing where extra strength is required.
However, it may be used alone where
tree size and structure prevent the use of
cable bracing. Only one rod will generally be required in a co-dominant stem

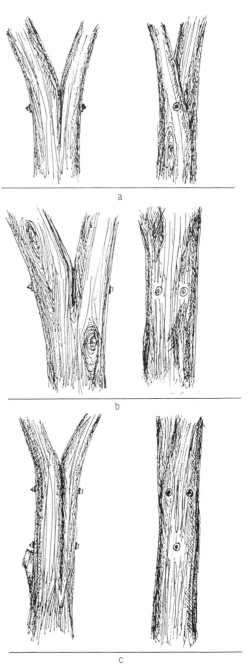

Figure 44   Rod bracing.
a Treatment of a small co-dominant stem with a single
rod brace.
b Two parallel rods installed just below the crotch,
approximately one-third of trunk diameter apart, where
excessive twisting forces may be encountered.
c Treatment for a long split and to prevent twisting in a
large diameter trunk.

of small diameter — say up to 450 mm diameter. Two parallel rods would normally be required where extensive twisting forces are expected. Tree shape, size and exposure to wind are all factors that must be considered. The rod or rods should be positioned at or just below the crotch. Where two parallel rods are installed these should generally be spaced approximately one-third of trunk diameter apart. For long splits in large diameter trunks an additional rod brace installed lower down the trunk may be required. The installation of rods in direct vertical alignment is not recommended as this practice can hinder the trees ability to compartmentalise the wounds. Rod bracing techniques are illustrated.

The old practice of fitting rods at varying heights above the crotch is also discouraged. Such rigid braces place excessive stress on the tree at the point of fitting. In gusty weather this can result in limb breakage or cause the rod to enlarge drill holes and damage callus tissue.

Rod bracing of cavities is of dubious value as it can disrupt the compartmentalisation process by breaching the barrier zone (referred to in 'Compartmentalisation of decay' under 'Tree growth and development') and spreading decay into sound wood.

Rod braces are also secured with nuts and recessed washers as described under 'Cable bracing'. Rod sizes should be selected to suit both trunk/stem diameter(s) and expected forces. Sizes of rod generally range from 10 to 25 mm diameter. It may be necessary to use custom-made rods, threaded at the ends only, for the bracing of especially large specimens.

Propping

Propping is a means of supporting low horizontal limbs when cable bracing is impractical. These circumstances may occur when the tree structure does not provide suitable anchor points to give adequate support when under load.

Figure 45   Propping — sometimes used to support low horizontal limbs as an alternative to cable bracing.

Props should be strong enough to support the expected loads and may be made from steel or durable timber. They should be located on a base (such as a concrete pad) of sufficient size to support them adequately and prevent them from sinking into soft ground. The saddle portion of a prop should be shaped to minimise bark damage, although some is inevitable, and padding of the saddle is unlikely to reduce this damage.

Tree
work procedures

In order to carry out most tree surgery operations it is necessary to gain access to the canopy of the tree. The equipment used for this purpose, climbing techniques and care of climbing equipment are discussed below.

Equipment

The various means of gaining access include elevated working platforms, ladders, and rope and harness.

Elevated working platforms

An elevated working platform consists of a man-carrying bucket attached to a boom which may be raised or lowered. These units are also known as 'travel towers' or 'cherry pickers'. They are widely used by organisations such as local government parks departments which are involved in large-scale street tree and park tree works programs. Cherry pickers are particularly useful for working on unsound and unstable trees that are too dangerous to climb.

A range of elevated working platforms is available, and it includes:

- self-propelled (generally three-wheeled) units with an approximate maximum platform height of 6 metres;
- trailer-mounted, trailed units with an approximate maximum platform height of 13 metres; and

- truck-mounted units (elevating platform vehicles) with an approximate maximum platform height of 30 metres.

Most tree surgery work can be carried out using an elevating platform, provided that the platform can gain access to the tree's canopy. Hydraulic and pneumatic pruning equipment can be fitted to these units. For many pruning operations, such as cleaning out, it may be difficult to reach all areas of the crown, particularly those close to the trunk and framework. This may lead to a poor standard of workmanship through imprecise placement and execution of pruning cuts; the problem is exacerbated by the use of long-handled hydraulic loppers and hydraulic chainsaws.

If not used properly, an elevating working platform can be dangerous. It should only be set up on firm ground, with minimal slope. In the case of truck-mounted (elevating platform vehicle) units, this slope should be a maximum of 5 degrees. Stabilisers must be used to reduce the slope if this is required to stabilise the machine. On unsealed surfaces, timber pads should be used in conjunction with the stabilisers to distribute the weight over a greater surface area. Wheels should be chocked and the parking brake must be applied to prevent the machine from running away.

Details of safe working practices when using elevating working platforms on roadways and near overhead powerlines may be obtained from local government and electrical supply authorities.

Figure 46 An elevated working platform commonly known as a 'travel tower' or 'cherry picker'.

a

Ladders

A ladder is generally used in arboricultural operations to gain initial access to a tree. It is then removed and the operator uses rope and harness. The use of a ladder as a work platform is not generally recommended.

Ladders should comply with appropriate safety standards. They should also be maintained carefully and when not in use stored out of the weather with stiles supported to prevent bowing. Suitable materials for ladders are steel, timber, aluminium or fibreglass. Timber ladders should be protected only with a clear coating of varnish so that it will not hide fractures in the wood. With the exception of fibreglass ladders, all types are capable of conducting electricity. Steel and aluminium ladders must not be used near electrical installations and timber ladders must only be used with care as there are wire strengtheners placed in the stiles.

Only use a ladder if it is erected on a firm, level and secure footing at a slope of not less than 1:4. Where necessary, another person may stand at the foot of the ladder to prevent it from slipping, except when cutting operations are in progress above. Not more than one person should be on a ladder at any time.

b

Figure 47 **a** and **b** Tree work sites. Note the use of warning signs and safety cones.

In rare situations where it may be necessary to use the ladder as a work platform (for instance when pruning a long, low horizontal limb with no suitable overhead anchor point for the climbing rope) extreme caution should be exercised. The top of the ladder should extend *well* beyond the supporting limb to allow for upward movement of the limb when its weight is reduced by the cutting operation. The ladder should be tied securely to the limb to prevent it being dislodged if struck by a cut limb or limb section. Further to this, the operator *must* be secured with a harness and pole strap around the limb.

Rope and harness (climbing) equipment

Rope Nylon rope is highly recommended as a lifeline for tree climbing, as it is the strongest man-made fibre rope available for this purpose. It will stretch to approximately 50% of its original length before breaking; this characteristic enables it to absorb some impact in the case of a fall. Also it is waterproof and rot-proof, and has a relatively high melting point (250°C) which is sufficient to withstand friction caused during normal climbing operations. Nylon rope used in tree climbing should be at least 12 mm in diameter and is usually of three-stranded or hawser-layed construction. Other types of rope construction, such as plaited or braided, are also used. Such rope should have a breaking load of 3000 kg, which gives a safe working load (SWL) of 500 kg. The SWL for personal safety equipment is calculated on a safety factor of one-sixth of the breaking load.

The life of nylon climbing rope depends on its quality and the conditions of use. For instance, rope used when climbing rough-barked trees, such as oaks (*Quercus* spp.), may have a shorter life than that used for climbing smooth-barked gums, such as Spotted Gum (*Eucalyptus maculata*). It should be remembered that nylon rope is subject to degradation by ultraviolet light, so it is recommended that this rope be stored in a dark place when not in use.

Only the best quality nylon rope should be used for climbing. It should be made of continuous-filament yarn with no knots in the fibres along its length. Nylon rope with a firm lay normally holds its shape better and is generally recommended, especially for heavier climbers. However, nylon ropes with soft lay may be better for lighter climbers as the prussik knot will grip more securely.

Normally, the length of the nylon rope used for climbing should be from a minimum of about 30 metres up to a maximum of about 50 metres. The ends of each climbing rope should be seized by whipping to prevent the rope from coming apart. Sailmaker's whipping should be used for this purpose. Back splicing is not recommended as it will increase the diameter of the rope ends, causing them to become caught in branch forks. Details of sailmaker's whipping are to be found in Appendix 1. The ends of synthetic fibre ropes can be heat sealed in addition to the whipping.

Nylon ropes that are no longer suitable for climbing may still be serviceable as lowering ropes, or they can be cut into short lengths for use as tool strops etc.

Harness A tree surgery harness or safety belt is intended for use as a suspended working seat. Such a harness is not efficient in arresting a fall; even a short fall (less than 1 metre) in such a harness can place an unacceptable load on the human body. Therefore, during normal use, *the harness should only be used by anchoring above the climber's body*, with the climber's weight in the harness, at all times.

Harnesses should be made of approved synthetic materials with a breaking strain and safe working load (SWL) equivalent to, or better than, that of the nylon rope being used as a lifeline. The harness consists of a **waist belt** and seat strap with **suspension D-rings** for attaching a **karabiner** and climbing rope. The waist belt also has D-rings to which a pole belt may be attached. This type of harness allows the climber to have both hands free for working, whilst being supported safely and in relative comfort.

A karabiner is usually used to attach the climbing rope to the suspension D-rings of the harness. A screwgate or twist lock karabiner with a breaking strain of at least 2500 kg is recommended. While karabiners of lesser breaking strains may be used for attaching tool strops to the harness, they should not be used for attaching a climbing rope. The karabiners used for attachment of a pole belt to a harness should also have a breaking strain of at least 2500 kg and a screw gate.

Pole belt A pole belt can be used in conjunction with a rope and harness for climbing trees. There are two types of pole belt available: synthetic webbing similar to harness material and braided steel wire rope. Although the steel type is safer when used in conjunction with chainsaws, it is better suited to spur climbing because of its rigidity.

Spurs Spurs may be used together with rope, harness and pole strap for tree removal operations. *They must not be used for normal tree surgery* as damage to the tree will result. Good quality climbing spurs have robust replaceable gaffs and adjustable shanks. Comfort and safety are design features of the best quality spurs. Examples of spurs with these features include Bashlin and Klein brands.

Climbing techniques

Rope and harness techniques are generally recommended for working in trees. These techniques are discussed below.

Figure 48 Checking a nylon climbing rope for damage and imperfections prior to climbing.

Preparation

Prior to climbing, the climbing rope must be checked for any damage or imperfections. This can be done when unflaking the rope and laying it at the base of the tree. It is important that the rope lies in irregular-sized coils so that it will pay out easily without tangling when climbing.

Before climbing, the operator must first put on a harness with the pole belt attached. When fitting the harness, the waist belt should be adjusted firmly so that it will not slip up from the waist, leaving the climber supported only

Figure 49 **a–c** Making a bight in a climbing rope prior to throwing into a tree.

under the armpits. Conversely, the harness should not be so tight that it restricts the climber's circulation.

Next the climber must get the rope up into the tree. To begin this procedure, several small coils and a **bight** are made at one end of the rope. This should enable that end of the rope to uncoil after being thrown over a strong limb as high as possible in the tree. To assist in throwing, it is usual to hold several loose coils in either hand. Where possible, right-handed people should hold the small coils and bight in the right hand and throw over the limb from their right (facing the trunk) to the left. The reverse is true for left-handed people.

Once over the limb, the rope now uncoiled is lowered sufficiently to provide at least one arms length of rope for passing through a karabiner (from left to right) in preparation for tying a bowline.

A **bowline** (left-hand) is then tied around the karabiner to secure the climbing rope to the harness. The bowline is commonly used and recommended as the best knot for this purpose. It may be untied with ease after having had a load placed on it. A figure-of-eight loop tied in the bight can also be used. Using the remaining tail portion of rope, a **prussik knot** is then tied to the rope hanging from the limb to ground (the standing part). The prussik knot grips the standing part of the rope, when weighted, to support the climber in ascent, descent or while working. This knot should not be tied too loosely otherwise it may not grip. If tied too tightly, it may 'lock up' and not provide sufficient movement during use.

A **figure-of-eight knot** should be tied in the tail of the rope left after making the prussik knot. This knot is tied as a safety measure, designed to prevent the tail slipping back through the prussik knot and spilling it.

Figure 50   **a–d** Throwing a climbing rope over a limb.

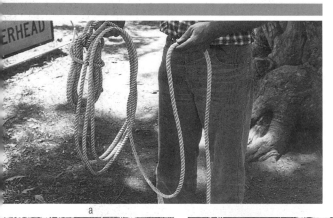

a

b   c   d

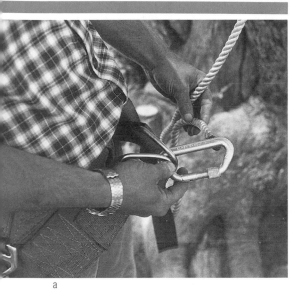

a

b

Figure 51 **a** and **b** Passing one arms length of climbing rope through a screwgate karabiner in preparation for tying a bowline. Note the correct arrangement of the harness 'D' rings and the karabiner.

a

b

c

d

Figure 52 **a–d** Tying a left-hand bowline to secure the climbing rope to the karabiner.

a

b

c

d

Figure 53   a–e Tying a prussik knot in a climbing rope.

Figure 54   Completed left-hand bowline, prussik knot and figure-of-eight knot.

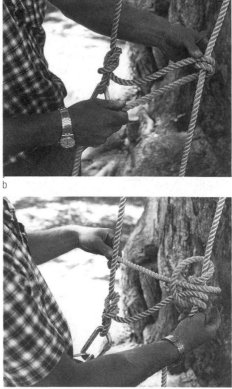

e

Ascending and descending

Before ascending the tree, re-check that the climbing rope karabiner is correctly attached, with the screwgate fully closed and the knots correctly tied. Note that a load

a

b

Figure 55 Ascending a tree using rope and harness.
a Pulling down on the standing part of the rope below the prussik knot.
b Sliding the prussik knot up to take slack out of the rope between the bowline and prussik knot.

Figure 56 Using a pole strap to secure the climber while changing anchor points. Pole strap secure around tree trunk **a** prior to untying knots and re-positioning the climbing rope **b**.

should be applied *only* to the *long axis* of a karabiner.

To ascend the tree, it is necessary to pull down on the standing part of the rope below the prussik knot, then slide the prussik knot up to take up the slack. To make these actions easier, the climber's buttocks should also be thrust upwards reducing weight on the harness and strain on the arms. These actions are repeated to ascend the tree. Climbing should be assisted by placing the feet against the tree trunk.

When it is necessary to change the position of the climbing rope, the climber should *remain attached to the tree at all times*. This may be done in one of two ways:

• by using a pole strap around the trunk or a limb before untying the knots and repeating the process above; or
• by throwing the other end of the climbing rope over a higher limb and tying a new set of knots before untying those supporting the climber.

a

b

A controlled descent is achieved by gently pulling down on the prussik knot. Fast descents should be avoided as the friction caused can be sufficient to melt the fibres of the climbing rope, especially inside the prussik knot.

Anchor points

When working in a tree, it is usual to choose the highest, most central anchor point, in order to achieve a narrow (acute) angle between the climber and the anchor point.

The climber's weight should be in the harness at all times, and the anchor point should always be above the climber.

If it is necessary to go above this anchor point *temporarily*, then a secondary method of attachment needs to be used, for example a pole strap.

The anchor point should be strong enough to support the climber, and large enough to minimise bark damage due to rope friction. The strength of an anchor point is influenced by the tree species, soundness of wood, and the nature of the fork. The climber's judgement in selecting anchor points will be influenced by experience and knowledge of tree species. If in doubt, 'err on the side of caution'.

To avoid undue damage to forks in thin of soft-barked species, an accessory climbing strop may be utilised at the anchor point. This may be constructed from a minimum of 12 mm diameter, or preferably larger diameter, nylon rope with a metal thimble spliced into an eye. Eye-splicing is shown in Appendix 2. This strop is fixed to the anchor point (using a running bowline) and the lifeline passed through the thimbled eye as illustrated.

Figure 57   An accessory strop used as an aid when climbing or lowering branches on soft-barked species. The strop comprises a thimbles eye secured by way of a running bowline.

Care of rope and harness (climbing equipment)

It is important that all climbing equipment is properly checked, serviced and stored before use.

When in use, care must be taken to keep rope free of hazardous material on the ground. Such material includes sandy, gritty and stony soil, mud, broken glass and other sharp materials. The primary danger of mud, sand and like is that these may be worked into the lay of the rope, thereby continuing to have an abrasive effect on the internal fibres during use. *Never walk or stand on ropes* as this will exacerbate the problem.

During tree surgery or removal operations it is the ground staff's responsibility to ensure that all rope is kept clear of debris on the ground and material being removed from the tree. Such material may not only damage the rope, but it may also become entangled and hinder operations. If rope becomes badly soiled, it should be washed in warm water with pure soap prior to being air dried (away from direct heat) and stored.

a

b

c

d

e

Figure 58 Flaking a climbing rope.
a–e The rope is pulled down from the tree over a branch. This enables it to be checked for damage. At the same time kinks and twists are removed. Flaking is completed by applying several frapping turns and securing the tail of the rope.

Climbing rope should be flaked while being pulled down from the tree; it can easily be checked for damage and twists, and kinks can be removed. A right-hand-lay rope should be coiled in a clockwise direction when flaking.

Harnesses and pole belts should be checked for cuts and abrasions that result in weakening of webbing and stitches. Like rope, harness should be kept clean and free of contamination.

Spurs should be checked and the gaffs sharpened with a fine flat file and maintained according to their designed original profile. Leather straps and pads can be treated occasionally with a leather dressing.

It is important that all climbing equipment is *stored in a dry area free from contaminants* such as chemicals, oil and fuel. Rope should be hung in flakes. Equipment such as ropes and harness should always be stored in a dark area to prevent degradation from ultraviolet light.

It is the individual operator's responsibility to check, service and store all climbing equipment properly before and after use. Any equipment suspected of being defective should not be used unless it has been tested and proved to be safe; where necessary, this equipment may need to be returned to the manufacturer for testing and repair. Equipment found to be defective, and not repairable, should be destroyed.

Rope and harness rescue techniques

While all arborists should work to current safe working practices, it only takes a momentary lapse of concentration for an accident to occur. The worst place for an accident is in a tree. A climber with a minor injury may still be able to descend unassisted and receive treatment, but where a serious accident has occurred, the climber will need to be rescued by other staff.

So that the climber can receive treatment and be rescued quickly and safely, each tree crew should have staff trained in first aid and practice tree rescues.

The actual method of rescuing an injured climber will depend on the size of the unit (i.e. how many staff are at the worksite) and also on the type of equipment available. It is worth considering some special items of equipment that should enable quicker and safer rescues to be carried out.

Procedures for rescues should be established and put in place as part of the normal work practice. It is essential that each crew has more than one competent climber working on the site. The workload can then be shared, lessening fatigue, and enabling one climber to be available on the ground to carry out a rescue if the climber in the tree should be injured.

As well as having an adequate first aid kit on site, and staff trained to use it, crews should also know where to find a telephone, the location of the worksite, how to gain access if this is not straightforward, and the phone numbers of all emergency services.

Aerial rescue procedures can be divided into three phases:

1 *The rescuer safely reaching the injured climber* An assessment of the dangers on the site needs to be made first. If working next to power lines, the tree may have become electrified due to contact with the electrical conductors, requiring the local electrical authority to be called in to disconnect the power supply before a rescue can commence. The rescuer should follow normal climbing safety precautions and not take any unnecessary risks.

2 *Application of first aid upon reaching the injured climber* Application of first aid may not be easy, as this will depend on the extent of injuries, position of the injured person in the tree and whether the injured is conscious.

3 *Establishment of the most suitable means of descending with the injured climber* Perhaps the simplest method of ensuring that a rescuer can quickly and safely gain access to a tree and reach an injured climber is always to set an extra climbing rope in the tree from an appropriate anchor point. In these emergency situations the use of climbing spurs to assist in reaching an injured climber may be justified as a life-saving measure despite the injury caused to the tree.

Each rescue will present a unique situation, as also will each tree and each arboricultural operation. Some possible rescue scenarios are outlined below.

- The rescuer and the injured climber each descend on their own ropes. The rescuer may also need to operate the prussik knot of the injured climber's rope.
- The injured climber's prussik knot may be untied enabling ground staff to lower the injured climber whilst the rescuer descends and assists as required.
- If the injured climber's rope is damaged, then both climbers could descend on the rescuer's rope. The injured climber would need to be attached to the bowline side of the rescuer's rope by a prussik loop or an ascender and sling. It may be necessary for the rescuer to cut the injured climber free from his own rope system after being attached to the rescuer's rope. Therefore, a sharp knife or secateurs should be carried by the rescuer.
- Another possibility, if the injured climber's rope has been damaged, is to have ground staff lower them both on the rescuer's rope.

An unconscious or severely incapacitated climber will need to be supported in an upright position. This may be achieved by placing a sling around the upper torso (under the arms) and attaching this to the rope on which he is being lowered. While it may be possible to improvise such slings in an emergency, it would be better to have some already made up and kept as part of the rescue equipment.

It must be stressed again that each tree crew needs to consider the possibility of accidents occurring to climbers, establish rescue procedures and practise them regularly, and maintain first aid skills.

Branch and tree removal

An important aspect of tree surgery work is the removal of trees and branches. This is carried out by selective pruning or, if necessary, by complete tree removal. The latter operation is the natural final phase of the complete tree management cycle which began years earlier with tree selection and planting.

There are many reasons for removing amenity trees and these include:

- trees being structurally unsound and dangerous;
- trees being potentially dangerous due to growth habit, environmental stresses, or damage by pests and diseases; and
- trees being potentially or actually damaging to buildings, property or other valuable plants due to undesirable root activity or shading.

As tree surgeons have the expertise, tools and equipment to climb safely and remove parts of trees, they are able to remove large unwanted trees safely when required. In situations where there is no access for heavy machinery such as elevating platform vehicles, a tree surgeon may be the only person capable of carrying out this work. A well managed tree removal is dependent on specialist skills, experience, a safe work method and a craftsman-like approach.

Safety

All branch and tree removal procedures are potentially very dangerous, so it is important that any person involved should learn the skills required under the supervision of an experienced operator.

Before new climbers are allowed to attempt branch or tree removal, they should first spend some time as a groundperson. This should enable them to learn rope management techniques, and gain a good appreciation of the forces applied to ropes when suspending and lowering cut branches and tree sections. This will also demonstrate the importance of planning the method and sequence of work, and promote efficient handling of cut sections by those on the ground. It must be emphasised that, before attempting these operations, members of the tree crew should be adequately trained in safe climbing techniques and be competent in the use of chainsaws through extensive training on the ground.

Eye protection, ear muffs, cut resistant chain-guard trousers or chaps and steel-capped safety boots should be worn when using chainsaws. High visibility clothing should also be worn in public areas. It is usual for the climber to direct ground staff in tree removal operations, so it is the *climber's responsibility to be aware of their safety at all times.*

During branch removal operations, *ground staff must wear approved safety helmets, and be equipped with robust leather gloves* for personal safety. Ground staff should position themselves well clear of cutting and lowering operations. It is imperative that they are skilled in rope handling procedures.

Ropes should:

- *not be wrapped around the hands or the body;*
- *be kept clear* of falling timber and sharp objects on the ground;
- *be kept free* of tangles and clear of obstructions; and
- *be moved in coils*, not dragged along the ground.

Ground staff also need to be aware of the safety of the climber, paying particular attention to the position of the climbing ropes relative to saws and falling timber.

Having taken all the above precautions, staff still need to be constantly aware of the possibility that members of the public may still attempt to enter the worksite, and may require firm but polite restraint. The use of signs, safety cones (*witches' hats*), ropes and parawebbing may be required to delineate the site adequately and isolate it from the public.

Ropes

Types and characteristics of ropes commonly used in branch or tree removal operations are set out in Table 8 below.

Manilla and other natural fibre ropes are generally cheap, and handle and knot well, but deteriorate if not stored and maintained correctly. These ropes have poor resistance to chemicals, and rot if not dried after use in wet conditions. Drying is achieved by flaking the rope and hanging it in a well-ventilated situation. A method of flaking is described under 'Tree work procedures'.

Nylon and polypropylene, being synthetic materials, do not rot but deteriorate in ultraviolet light and should be stored away from direct sunlight. Although these ropes are resistant to many chemicals and oils, every care should be taken to prevent contamination by any substance as damage to the rope may not be apparent.

External wear of the rope does not always give an accurate indication of the extent of deterioration. In particular, with nylon climbing rope, the outer fibres will become 'furry' with normal use, adding useful abrasion resistance to the rope. A useful test to determine the extent of deterioration in a rope is to open up the lay at various points along its length and check for any powdering or dusting between the strands. When this is present, the rope should be *destroyed*.

Table 8   Properties of ropes (all values are approximate)

Type of rope	Diameter (mm)	Breaking load (kg)	SWL* (kg)	Stretch (%)	Melting point (°C)
Manilla (A Grade)	12	1070	178	N/A	N/A
	16	2030	338		
	24	4570	761		
Polypropylene	12	2030	338		
	16	2500	586	28	165
	24	7600	1266		
Nylon	12	3000	500	50	250
	(usually recycled climbing rope)				

* Safe working load based on a factor of 6 as recommended.

Branch removal

If only removing individual branches from a tree, a knowledge of the correct placement of the final pruning cuts is assumed. Undercutting branch sections to prevent bark tearing may also be required. Refer to 'Pruning' for further details.

When the area below the tree is free from obstructions, cut branches and branch sections can simply be allowed to fall. If necessary, stacked branch wood can be utilised to protect lawns, paths etc. When branches or branch sections are too large or heavy for the climber to hold and throw clear, or obstructions prevent their free falling, then lowering ropes are used. It is usual to lower branches or branch sections by passing a lowering rope, of sufficient strength, through a suitable anchor point and then attaching it to the branch being removed.

When selecting suitable anchor points for a lowering rope the climber must consider the weight of branch sections to be lowered, as well as any shock loadings. The position of the anchor point should also promote the efficient lowering and handling of the section by ground staff. When working in thin- or soft-barked trees, except in the case of complete tree removal, it may be necessary to run lowering ropes through a suitably sized anchor strop, similar to the one discussed under 'Anchor points' in the chapter 'Tree work procedures'.

The descent of heavy branches or branch sections is controlled by introducing friction into the rope system — usually by the ground staff taking one or more turns of the lowering rope(s) around the trunk of the tree.

Hitches and knots recommended for the purpose of lowering cut tree sections include the timber hitch and half hitch, round turn and two half hitches, and running bowline. A clove hitch with half hitches is also used by some arborists for branch lowering, but this may become jammed and difficult to untie if a

a

b

Figure 59 **a** and **b** Branch lowering operation. Note anchor points and control of lowering ropes.

sudden load is applied, so it cannot be recommended.

It is essential that ground staff are also proficient in the use of other knots, such as the sheet bend, marline spike hitch, bowline bend and bowline, as these knots are fundamental to branch removal operations. The knots and their uses are described on the following pages.

The tie-off point on a branch will be selected to suit the work requirements. It is most common to attach lowering ropes to the butt (trunk) end of a branch, this being close to the climber and, therefore, easy to reach and tie off. This presumes that there is enough free space below the branch to allow the head to swing down without causing damage or becoming entangled.

Alternatives to this method are:

- using a single lowering rope tied off at the balance point of the branch — this method requires personnel to make an accurate assessment of the actual balance point, a skill which requires experience; or
- using two lowering ropes, one tied to the butt end and one at the head — excellent control of the branch can be achieved with this method by either lowering the butt end first, or the head end first, or both simultaneously.

It may be desirable to use another rope as a pulling rope to direct the descent of

Figure 60   Marlin spike hitch.

the branch or branch section. This may require more than one ground person. With lightweight material, the climber may be able to control the lowering rope, allowing the ground person to operate the pull rope.

As all these methods offer good control of the cut branch or branch section, the one selected will depend on the particular situation. Obviously, the more ropes required, the longer the operation will take.

Knots and hitches

The **marlin spike hitch** is used for attaching tools to ropes for the climber to pull up into the tree. Sufficient weight in the tail of the rope is essential to prevent the marlin spike hitch from coming undone, so this knot should not be tied in the end of a rope. When tying a tool at or near the end of a rope, a bowline should be used instead.

The **sheet bend** is used for joining ropes, generally of different diameters, for example when attaching a lowering

Figure 61   Sheet bend.

a

b

Figure 62 **a** and **b** Bowline tied in the end of a rope for lowering of tools.

rope or a tool line to a climbing rope for the climber to pull it up into the tree. This knot remains secure without being so tight that it becomes difficult to untie.

The **bowline** (right-hand) is especially suitable for tying tools onto the end of ropes such as tool lines. When tied as an end knot, a **right-hand** bowline (as illustrated) should be used.

The **bowline bend** is suitable for joining two ropes to which a load will be applied. The knot consists of two bowlines.

The **timber hitch** is often used for lowering heavy limbs. When tied, it should have at least three turns tucked with the lay of the rope and spread evenly around the circumference of the branch. On smooth-barked branches, and where there is no stub to hold the timber hitch in place, a **half hitch** should be made before tying the timber hitch. This will be more secure than a timber hitch alone. The timber hitch is not suitable for use with synthetic ropes as these will stretch under load and spill the knot or cause it to slip.

Figure 63 Bowline bend.

Figure 64 Timber hitch.

Figure 65   Round turn and two half hitches.

Figure 66   Running bowline.

Generally, the **round turn and two half hitches** is used for lowering smaller limbs than those requiring a timber hitch or running bowline.

The **running bowline** is especially useful for securing the head of a branch which is to be lowered but is out of reach. In this procedure, the end of the rope is thrown over the point where the knot is to be tied and the tail is then retrieved. This is used to tie a running bowline knot around the standing part of the rope. The knot is then pulled tight to secure the branch for lowering, and after use it can be untied with ease.

Trunk removal

Where an entire tree is to be removed in sections, the branches should be removed

a

b

Figure 67   **a** and **b** Use of pole belt, climbing rope and spurs in a trunk removal operation.

as described above before beginning work on the trunk.

From this point on, it is usual for the climber to use a pole strap to secure himself to the tree as there will no longer be a usable anchor point above the working position. It may also be necessary to use climbing spurs, because of the lack of branch stubs for the climber to stand on. It is important that *the climbing spurs fit correctly* when in use. The lengths of the shanks should be adjusted to suit the individual and the straps fastened quite firmly before the climber ascends. As a secondary safety measure, a climbing rope should be looped around the trunk and tied to the karabiner in the normal manner with bowline, prussik and figure-of-eight knots. This should be secured *below* the pole strap to ensure that the climber will still be tied on should the pole strap be cut accidentally. It should also allow a fast, safe and comfortable descent if the climber is injured or needs to descend for some other reason.

The first phase of trunk removal is 'taking out' the top of the tree. Where space allows, the top of the tree may be free felled with a directional scarf and back cut. If necessary, a pull rope can be used to aid the direction of the fall. Where there is insufficient space, the **snatching** technique described below may be used. Further details regarding the directional scarfing and back cutting techniques are to be found under 'Directional falling' later in this chapter.

Depending on the situation, further sectional removal of the trunk may be carried out by either free falling in sections or snatching. These procedures are described below.

Free falling in sections

Where space allows, different techniques may be employed to free fall the trunk in *manageable* sections.

It is possible to dismantle the trunk in suitably sized blocks that may be either pushed, pulled, dropped or slid from the trunk, one after another. These four methods are shown and described below. As in branch removal, branch wood can be stacked at the base of the tree for cushioning the falling trunk sections. This cushioning not only protects lawns, paths and so on, but also prevents large sections from rolling.

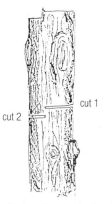

Figure 68a   Trunk section showing free falling. Method 1: Two staggered horizontal cuts.

Method 1 is only suitable for small diameters (150–200 mm). It is not recommended for larger trunk sections; methods 2–4 are more appropriate treatments for these. Method 1 uses two successive staggered horizontal cuts. The first cut is made to about three-quarters of the way through the trunk, and the second staggered cut is made about one-quarter of the way through. After cutting, the section is forcibly broken off and thrown clear.

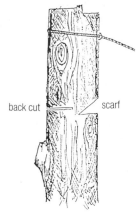

Figure 68b   Trunk section showing free falling. Method 2: Directional scarf and back cut with pull rope.

Method 2 provides for the use of a directional scarf and back cut as described under 'Directional falling'. On completion of cutting, the chainsaw is turned off and secured on the tool strop. The small hinge of wood left between the scarf and back cut enables the section to be felled clear in the direction of the scarf. This may be accomplished either by the climber pushing it or by ground staff pulling a rope secured around the section. A pull rope provides better control, particularly on larger sections and where trunk lean is encountered.

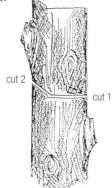

cut 2

cut 1

Figure 68c   Trunk section showing free falling. Method 3: Horizontal cut and sloping back cut.

Method 3 provides good control in falling of cut sections of straight, upright stems. This method consists of an initial horizontal cut, about three-quarters of the way through the trunk, and a second cut made down at an angle to intersect the first. The chainsaw is turned off after the second cut is completed. This allows the chainsaw to be removed from the second cut, leaving the section to sit flat on the trunk. It may then be pushed off, pulled off, or lifted and thrown clear.

Method 4 comprises one sloping cut.

Figure 68d   Trunk section showing free falling. Method 4: Downward sloping cut.

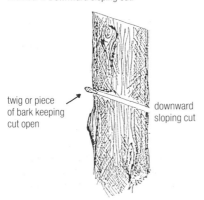

twig or piece of bark keeping cut open

downward sloping cut

To prevent chainsaw jamming and bar pinching, especially on larger sections, pieces of twig or bark may be inserted in the kerf when halfway through the cut. This cut should be finished quickly so the section can slide clear of the chainsaw freely. It should be noted that as the chainsaw will still be running when the section slides clear, the utmost caution is required.

Snatching

Snatching is a technique by which sections of the trunk or branch are lowered individually from an anchor point below each section.

It is important to realise that the strain on the rope system using this technique is much greater than in all other branch

Figure 69   Trunk removal by snatching.
a Timber hitch and half hitch above scarf and half hitch below.
b Timber hitch and half hitch above scarf and lowering rope reeved through a thimbled strop below.

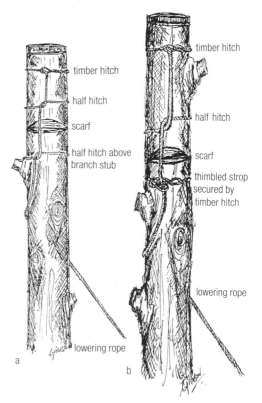

timber hitch

timber hitch

half hitch

half hitch

scarf

scarf

half hitch above branch stub

thimbled strop secured by timber hitch

lowering rope

lowering rope

a

b

or trunk removal operations. Therefore, it is vital to select ropes that are of sufficient strength.

The procedure by which each section is treated is given below.

- Scarf the section in the desired direction of fall.
- Half hitch the lowering rope below the section and above a branch stub. If there is no branch stub below the scarf, attach a suitable strop using a timber hitch or running bowline, reeve the rope through the thimbled eye of the strop, and tie a half hitch and timber hitch above the scarf.
- Tie off the section with a half hitch and a timber hitch. Alternatively, a running bowline may be substituted for the timber hitch; a running bowline *must* be used for a *nylon* lowering rope. Remove all slack from the rope before continuing. *There should be no slack between the knots.*
- The ground staff must secure the lowering rope by taking one or more turns around the trunk. The amount of friction that must be applied by the ground staff to hold and lower the cut section safely is determined by the weight of the section being removed.
- Back cut the section leaving a small hinge of holding wood.
- The section is then pushed over by the climber or pulled off with a pull rope used by the ground staff. The climber may wish to descend beforehand if the pull rope is used for this purpose.

This sequence is continued for each of the remaining trunk sections until the trunk is removed, or reduced sufficiently to enable the butt to be felled safely.

Directional falling

Where space and safety permit a tree may be felled in one piece. This is known as 'directional falling'. This is a large subject, but some aspects are discussed here. Further details can be found in texts including those listed in 'References and further reading' under 'Tree falling, trimming and crosscutting'.

Before the falling operation begins, many factors need to be considered. The nature of the worksite will dictate the precautions which must be taken to ensure the safety of both the operators and the public. In urban areas where directional falling may be carried out, for example in parks, recreational reserves, golf courses etc., the site safety requirements will be designed to isolate the public from the worksite. Ropes, parawebbing or other temporary fences should be erected at a distance of at least twice the height of the tree in all directions.

Warning signs indicating that tree falling is in operation should also be erected.

When the site is secure, the main emphasis on safety is directed towards the operators and work methods. Only the staff actually involved in the falling of the tree should be within the fenced off area, or at least two tree lengths from the tree being felled.

The first thing the operator must establish is the structural condition of the tree. Severe basal rot will indicate extreme caution and the tree may require special techniques due to the lack of sound wood to support and direct it as it falls. Consider using elevating platform vehicles for dismantling such trees in sections, as this may be the only safe way to proceed. Structural defects may be detected by looking for the presence of fungal brackets and/or cavities, by striking the trunk with an axe and listening for a hollow sound, or by boring into the trunk with a chainsaw or auger and examining the swarf for signs of decayed wood. Special electronic instruments may also be used for this purpose, for example the PIRM or Shigometer (see Appendix 4).

Having established that the tree is sound, the direction of fall can be determined by assessing the lean of the tree, weight distribution of the crown, wind direction, open space and other factors. The presence of neighbouring trees, especially if their canopies have grown together, should also be noted. Ground must be clear around the base of the tree to allow safe movement. There must be a clear escape route available to the faller at a 45° diagonal away from the proposed line of fall.

Standard falling techniques

Trees with no lean and an even weight distribution can be felled by using a standard 45° **scarf** and back cut on a calm day (or when the wind is blowing in the direction of the fall).

The scarf allows the tree to fall. It is made by placing two intersecting cuts in the tree at right angles to the desired direction of fall. This can be judged by lining up the direction of fall with the sight line on the chainsaw. *The scarf should be cut sufficiently deep into the tree so that the maximum width of hinge, consistent with tree shape and size, leaves sufficient uncut wood to make the back cut safely and place wedges.* Usually this entails making the scarf one-quarter to a maximum of one-third of trunk diameter deep. It is *essential* that the two scarf cuts do not overlap, to preserve the integrity of the **holding wood** (**hinge**). The effect of overlapping cuts at the point of the scarf is to lessen or negate the function of the hinge, causing a partial or total loss of control over the direction of fall. Apart from the damage resultant from the loss of control, the safety of all personnel, especially the faller, is put at risk.

The fall is completed by making the **back cut**. This can be made by cutting from the back of the tree towards the scarf, leaving a hinge of holding wood. However, the 'plunge cut and back release' method of falling as described for trees with heavy forward lean (below) is also recommended, particularly on fast growing trees and certain species with a tendency to split vertically when backcutting. Chainsaw cutter bars are less likely to be jammed when using the plunge cut

Figure 70   **a** and **b** A directional falling operation. Note the use of personal safety equipment and provision of clear 'escape routes'.

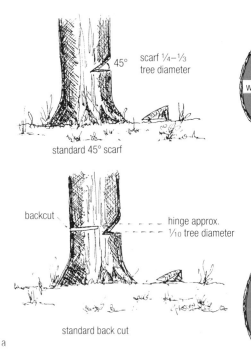

scarf ¼–⅓ tree diameter

45°

standard 45° scarf

backcut

hinge approx. ⅟₁₀ tree diameter

standard back cut

a

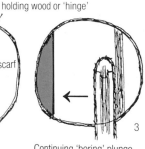

holding wood or 'hinge'

wood to be back cut

scarf

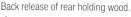

1 Beginning of plunge cut using lower quadrant of guide bar tip.

3 Continuing 'boring' plunge cut once guide bar tip is well surrounded by timber. This cut is plunged through the tree to establish the holding 'hinge' wood, then continue rearwards to establish the rear holding wood.

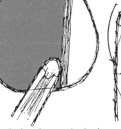

2

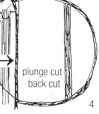

Back release of rear holding wood.

plunge cut back cut

4

Continuing plunge cut using lower quadrant of guide bar tip and pivoting saw.

b

and back release method. *The back cut should be placed at least one-tenth of the trunk diameter above the bottom scarf cut and parallel to it.* Back cutting should be completed on the safe side of the tree, taking high ground and canopy into consideration.

A falling wedge or wedges should be placed in the back cut as soon as it is deep enough for them to work without fouling the chainsaw cutter bar. These will prevent the tree sitting back on the cutter bar if lean has been miscalculated, and may assist the fall by being driven in to lift the tree. Plastic or aluminium alloy wedges are used for this purpose. A steel wedge *must not* be used as it will severely damage the saw chain if they make contact. This can also result in injury to the faller.

Figure 71   Directional falling — back cutting techniques.
a Standard 45° scarf and standard back cut.
b Plunge cut and back release method of back cutting (also Figure 72b).
c Stump of felled tree. Note scarf, hinge wood and back cut with step.

c

The remaining hinge will then control and direct the falling tree. *The standard hinge should be about one-tenth of the trunk diameter thick.* The step created by positioning the back cut above the bottom scarf cut will add to the effectiveness of the hinge and helps to prevent the butt of the falling tree from kicking backwards over the stump.

When the tree begins to fall the operator should stop the chainsaw and move back along the escape route well away from the stump. It is important to watch the tree as it falls, as debris may be projected back from other trees if struck. Other potential hazards such as branches broken in surrounding trees can also be noted.

Alternative falling techniques

These are used in various situations described below.

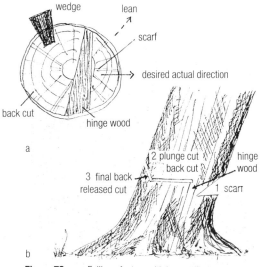

Figure 72   **a** Falling of a tree with heavy side lean. Note thicker hinge wood opposite side of lean.
b Plunge cut and back release method of falling for tree with heavy forward lean.

Trees with a side lean (or uneven weight distribution) can be felled using a tapered hinge back cut and wedge. This procedure begins with a standard scarf always placed in the desired direction of fall. The back cut is begun as usual, but more holding wood is left on the side opposite the lean. The wedge is placed on the lean side of the tree, at right angles to the lean, as soon as the back cut is deep enough to allow the wedge to work without fouling the cutter bar. *Never stand under the lean to make the back cut.* If the side lean is too extreme to allow this technique, it may be necessary to use a hand or power winch, or reduce the crown as required to even up the weight distribution.

Trees with a heavy forward lean may split up the trunk, due to tension, if felled using a standard back cut. For such trees, the back cut is begun by making a **plunge cut** (boring cut) to establish the holding wood, and then continuing this cut towards the back of the tree, leaving sufficient uncut wood to support the tree. The saw is removed from the plunge cut and the fall is completed by severing the uncut wood with a downward **back release cut** from the rear, using an axe or chainsaw.

When using plunge cutting to perform this operation, there is a serious risk of kickback. The cut must begin by using the bottom section of the nose of the cutter bar and cutting carefully at an angle towards the direction in which the boring cut is required. Continue cutting at this angle until the cut has a depth of about one to two widths of the cutter bar, then gradually pivot the chainsaw till the cutter bar is boring straight into the tree. *A good stance and firm grip* on the chainsaw is necessary when plunge cutting. By operating the chainsaw at full throttle, there should be less possibility of the chain snagging. Chainsaws fitted with large radius bars and safety chain are also less likely to cause kickback. Since the chainsaw tends to move forward when cutting, it is also a good idea to begin the plunge cut short of the holding wood.

Smaller trees which lean directly away from the desired line of fall can, with experience, be tipped against the lean with the aid of a falling bar or wedges. A shallow scarf, approximately one-quarter of the trunk diameter, will enable a wedge to be inserted into the back cut behind the chainsaw cutter bar, before the tree 'settles'. This should prevent jamming of the bar and chain. It is essential that the wedge or falling bar is 'working' in the *wood* of the tree so it may be necessary to use an axe to remove thick bark near the kerf.

Larger trees may require the use of hand or power winches, as described in the chapter 'Stump treatment', to pull them against their natural lean. In some cases it may be necessary to remove part or all of the tree in sections.

Hung-up or suspended trees

Trees which have lodged in other trees are referred to as 'hung-up' or 'suspended' trees. These may occur as the result of a tree falling mishap or when trees are windthrown during a storm. A hung-up tree is obviously a hazard in any situation, and it should be brought down as soon as possible. Where it is not possible to do this immediately, the tree and the danger zone around it should be isolated by erecting warning signs and, in urban areas, by erecting a suitable barrier such as parawebbing. At night it may also be necessary to use flashing hazard warning lights.

Never climb a hung-up tree or work under a 'hang-up'. It should be assumed that the tree may fall at any time. Also, it is not safe to attempt to bring down a hung-up tree by cutting sections off the butt in the hope that it will drop and fall clear.

When it is necessary to dismantle the hung-up tree in sections, the supporting tree, or another adjacent tree, may be used for climbing and anchorage. In some situations and where access permits, cranes and elevating platform vehicles can be a safe and efficient means of assisting removal. Where space permits, and no damage will be done in the surrounding area, hand or power winches may be used to pull out hung-up trees. It may be possible to use heavy lifting equipment if it is available. A winch or pull rope may be attached to the head of the tree to lift it and pull it clear, or attached to the butt to snig it out. The latter method

is likely to result in considerable damage to the supporting tree.

Further details on winching are to be found under 'Stump treatment'.

Windthrows

Windthrown trees, which are lying on the ground and are not hung-up, should be dealt with initially by crosscutting the trunk as close as possible to the root crown. This is done to reduce the danger of trunk movement, should the root system fall back into place. The root system may be propped, or the hole backfilled to prevent the roots from falling back into place when the trunk is cut off. This may be useful if the stump is to be removed.

Trimming and crosscutting

Figure 73   Trimming and crosscutting.

Having successfully and safely felled a tree, there are still many potential dangers which can be encountered while trimming

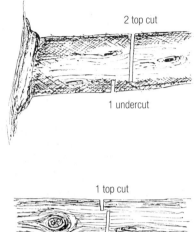

a

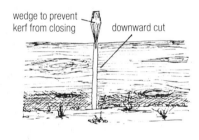

b

c

Figure 74   Crosscutting techniques.
a Branch supported by attachment to trunk only.
b Branch supported at both ends.
c Heavy log lying on the ground.

and crosscutting. These include chainsaw kickback, limbs held under tension whipping towards the operator when cut, and trees rolling when supporting limbs are cut. If safe working practices are adopted, these potential dangers can be reduced or eliminated. When on sloping ground, work from the higher-ground side of the tree wherever possible. This is particularly important when removing the last of the supporting limbs. It may be neces-

sary to chock the tree prior to cutting major supporting limbs and when crosscutting the trunk into sections.

When trimming fallen trees, it is usual to work from the butt towards the crown. In the case of large spreading trees, much of the crown may be held off the ground and it is advisable to deal with the crown first, provided that the tree is firmly supported and will not move or roll while this work is carried out.

It is safest to allow only one operator to work on trimming a fallen tree at any one time. There is considerable risk involved if several operators are cutting supporting limbs simultaneously.

The operator must learn to analyse the forces exerted on and by limbs and be able to determine whether wood is held in **compression** or **tension**. If a limb is cut from the tension side, it may whip towards the operator when released, and either inflict injury or be the cause of a chainsaw injury. Limbs supported at the butt will need to be top cut, and those supported at the tip will need to be undercut. Large limbs can be cut in sections to reduce tension progressively.

Some chainsaw trimming and crosscutting techniques are described below.

Large branches supported by attachment to the trunk only or trunk sections supported at one end only should be undercut and then severed with a top cut.

Large branches or trunk sections supported at both ends should be top cut and then severed with an undercut.

Trunk sections supported along their entire length (lying on the ground) and capable of being rolled may have a series of top cuts made through most of their diameter. These can be completed after the log is rolled. A cant hook can be used to assist in rolling the log. This procedure reduces the possibility of striking the ground with the saw chain.

Heavy logs supported along their entire length (lying on the ground) can be top cut and a plastic wedge inserted to prevent the kerf from closing and pinching the chainsaw cutter bar. In this situation the operator must be particularly careful not to strike the ground with the chainsaw and blunt it.

Treatment of prunings, branchwood and timber

An important part of many arboricultural operations is the removal of prunings and cut timber, especially when carrying out tree removals where this may be a significant part of the job. The method employed will depend on the scale of the operation, the site, the equipment available, and any restrictions such as local council by-laws or Government legislation.

Large volumes of waste material will be most easily and efficiently handled by using heavy equipment wherever access and site conditions permit. Such equipment could range from front-end loaders to purpose-built log-loading tractors and bulldozers. These are most suited to unrestricted sites where material can be heaped up for treatment or removal.

In urban areas it is usual for waste material to be cut to sizes which can be handled manually or with small machinery such as skid-steer loaders. Branchwood chippers or hoggers greatly reduce the volume of this material and are essential in areas where great distances must be travelled to remove and dispose of such materials. These machines also have the advantage of producing a useful product which can be recycled as garden mulch. Operators using chippers must have hearing protection because of high noise levels. It is possible that there may be restrictions on the hours during which such noisy machines may be operated, so check with the local council before operating one in a built up area.

Where material is not treated on site it may be removed in a truck, trailer or industrial waste bin. The removal of material by road must comply with the relevant road regulations, which include a requirement that loads be secured properly. In certain situations the use of netting over the load will be necessary,

Figure 75   Municipal tree pruning crew using an elevating platform vehicle (EPV) and branchwood chipper.

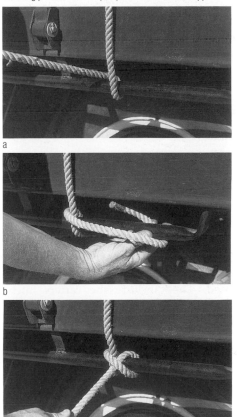

a

b

c

Figure 76   a–c Tying a clove hitch.
This knot is used to secure a rope to a rail at the start and finish of tying down a load.

but using a rope to tie down the load is generally sufficient. The advantages and disadvantages of various types of rope have been discussed previously. Recycled branch ropes or climbing ropes are often used for tying down loads.

The hitches used for securing loads can vary according to the type of rope used. They include the carters hitch, marline spike hitch and variations of the sheep shank for applying tension and the clove hitch for tying off to a rail. If using synthetic rope, sheep shank-like hitches are preferred because they are less likely to spill.

Figure 77   Tying down a load with a sheep shank like hitch.

Stump treatment

The final facet of the tree removal process is stump treatment, which may entail leaving the stump *in situ* or removing it.

Leaving stumps *in situ*

Leaving stumps *in situ* may be a practical choice for reasons such as lack of access for machinery, the possibility of damage being caused to other plants or structures, or when removal may cause an unnecessary increase in the cost of the job. These stumps should be cut as close to the ground as possible, unless otherwise requested, and they may then be camouflaged by appropriate landscaping.

Plants which produce **epicormic** regrowth from the cut stump can be treated chemically or manually. Plants with **suckering** root systems are best treated by chemical means. Manual treatment entails persistent removal of all shoots until the stump no longer produces regrowth. Chemical treatments are the cut stump and frill/stem injection methods described below.

To treat a cut stump it is necessary to apply herbicide only to the phloem area, so a paint brush or plastic squeeze bottle may be used. For best results, apply the herbicide *immediately* after the stump has been cut. At this time, intake by the vascular system should be rapid.

Frill/stem injection treatments entail making holes or incisions into the phloem tissue at intervals around the trunk, and applying a herbicide. This treatment is best carried out in the growing season before removing the tree. It is recommended for the treatment of species prone to root suckering, such as elms (*Ulmus* spp.) and poplars (*Populus* spp.). Where frill treatments are made, best results should be gained by treating at intervals rather than entirely, around the trunk as this will achieve better translocation of the herbicide. Similarly, frill treatment of standing trees will usually be more effective than treatment of cut stumps, as the herbicide should be translocated more effectively.

Herbicides suitable for direct application to stumps and trees include picloram, triclopyr and glyphosate. All are translocated throughout the plant, including the root system. As these herbicides are capable of killing a range of broadleaf plant species, great care is required when using them. It is important to note that in situations where roots of neighbouring plants come in contact with the roots of treated plants the non-target species can be affected. In the case of picloram it has been known for this to occur at quite a distance from the point of treatment. *Spillage of picloram and triclopyr on the soil and wind drift must be avoided* since such herbicides are soil residual and vapours can be carried by wind.

Careful thought should be given to the use of herbicides, particularly in garden situations. *Read and follow all directions and safety precautions on the product label before use.*

Stump removal

Where stump removal is required, the methods available include hand grubbing or the use of stump grinding machines and other heavy machinery.

In most situations stump removal is desirable for reasons of hygiene, for instance, trees planted in recently cleared soil infected with Armillaria root rot fungi (*Armillaria* spp.) may also become infected by this fungus. Prevention entails careful removal of all infected plant material, cultivation and soil fumigation prior to planting.

Hand grubbing is a laborious means of removing stumps, but it can be practical and cost effective, particularly for removing those which are small or inaccessible to machinery. If a stump is to be hand grubbed, it is best to cut it as high as possible to allow for maximum leverage when pushing or pulling. Then trench around the stump and cut all roots in the process. It can then be pulled (winched) or pushed out, while anchor roots and roots on the side away from the winch are cut away if necessary.

A range of anchors can be made or purchased for use when winching, but other trees are often used. Whatever

anchor is used for winching, it is most important that it is sufficiently strong and secure for the job in hand. To minimise strain on the anchor, the winch cable should be secured as low as possible.

Figure 78   Winching.
A Tirfor winch set up for winching with a wide webbing sling securing it to an anchor tree.

Figure 79   **a** and **b** Stump grinder in operation.

If other trees on the worksite are used as anchor points for a winch, they need to be protected from injury. A wide nylon or terylene webbing sling is ideal for securing the winch to an anchor tree.

Where a very large stump is pulled over, backfilling the stump hole should take place immediately to prevent the stump slipping back into the stump hole when the winch is released.

Heavy machinery can also be used for removing stumps. Although the means employed are different from hand grubbing, the principles are the same for the removal of difficult stumps, that is trenching and cutting around the root system and using a high point of attachment for pushing or pulling.

Stump grinders of various sizes and brands are also commonly used for removing stumps. This equipment is often the most cost-effective means of removing difficult stumps in situations such as home gardens where access is possible. These purpose-built machines are available from specialist contractors. Care must be taken as stump grinders can cause damage to underground services; check if there is a risk before using such machinery.

Chainsaw servicing and safety

It is always a serious problem to have breakdowns on the job, and this is particularly true of chainsaw failure when working on trees. To prevent breakdowns, chainsaws must be serviced properly and as specified by the manufacturer. Every chainsaw operator should be able to carry out basic servicing, details of which can be found in the owner's manual. Repairs to motor and electrical components often require special equipment and detailed mechanical knowledge so are usually better left to a specialist.

In this chapter, details of basic chainsaw servicing are provided. The maintenance schedules are based on a regular average daily engine operating time of 6–8 hours. However, when working in particularly dirty or dusty conditions, or when cutting *dry* timber, the service intervals may need to be shortened.

For safety reasons, before most of the maintenance procedures described are attempted, the ignition switch should be in the 'off' position.

Chainsaw maintenance

Daily maintenance

Maintenance tasks that should be carried out *each day* include the following:

- clean the air filter and air pre-filter;
- clean the air intake vents and chainsaw body;
- remove and clean the sprocket cover and chainbrake mechanism;
- check that the chain brake operates properly;
- clean and turn over the guide (cutter) bar;
- fill the fuel and chain oil tanks; and
- check and tighten all accessible screws and nuts.

These procedures are described below.

Air filter and air pre-filter   These should be dismantled and cleaned prior to use. Before removing the air filter, ensure that the choke butterfly is closed to prevent foreign matter entering the carburettor.

Flock filters and the pre-filter can be washed in clean petrol or in warm water and detergent (and rinsed clean), or blown clean with compressed air. After washing, the filter should be thoroughly dried before use. Having a second air filter available is recommended, so that one can be used while the other is drying. This also ensures that a clean filter is always available. Care should be taken when using compressed air as too high a pressure may blow the flock out of the filter. Damaged air filters must be replaced. Paper element filters should be maintained and replaced in accordance with the manufacturer's specification.

As powerful modern chainsaws rely heavily upon the intake of large amounts of air to function well, the maintenance of filters is a most important procedure.

Figure 80   Air pre-filter cleaning.

a

b

Air intake vents and body parts   The air intake vents and the saw body must be kept clean and free of obstructions. This will ensure that an adequate supply of cool air is flowing over the engine cylinder cooling fins.

Body parts can be cleaned with a small brush using kerosene or petrol. Two-stroke mix is not recommended as it will leave an undesirable oil residue. These solvents are highly flammable and care should be taken with their use. Work in an adequately ventilated area, keep the solvents away from naked flames, and allow washed parts to dry completely before starting the chainsaw.

A clean saw not only dissipates heat more efficiently, but also indicates the professional attitude of a craftsperson who takes care of his or her tools.

Only plastic or wooden scrapers should be used for removal of built up resins and sawdust from the motor and body parts. The use of screwdrivers or other metal objects is not recommended as these will damage paintwork, sometimes leading to corrosion, and may also damage engine parts.

Sprocket cover, chain brake and guide (cutter) bar   These must be *removed* for cleaning. Oil and sawdust should be thoroughly cleaned from the sprocket cover,

c

Figure 81   **a–c** Air filter cleaning.

Figure 82   Sprocket cover removed for cleaning.

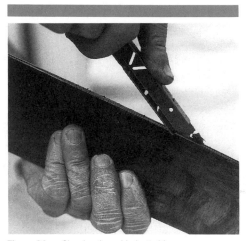

Figure 84   Cleaning the guide (cutter) bar groove.

a

b

Figure 83   **a** and **b** Cleaning a sprocket mounted chain brake.

chain brake, activating mechanism, and saw body. Particular attention should be given to the oil-feed hole in the saw body which supplies oil to the guide bar. After cleaning and re-assembly the chain brake should be checked to see that it operates properly. If the chainsaw has a chain brake mounted in the sprocket cover, it is critical that it is cleaned regularly and that the mechanism is checked.

The *guide (cutter) bar groove* should be scraped clean. Special tools are available for this purpose. Always clean from the tip of the bar, backwards. The oil inlet holes on the bar, which line up with the oil-feed hole, must be *thoroughly* cleaned to allow adequate oil supply to the guide bar and chain. When refitting the bar to the saw it should be turned over to equalise wear.

If the guide bar is fitted with a sprocket nose bearing, and where provision is made it should be greased with a high temperature grease using the special grease gun for this purpose.

Fuel and chain-oil tanks The tanks should be filled at the end of each day's work. This will minimise condensation of water in the tanks during storage. Only the two-stroke fuel mixture recommended by the chainsaw manufacturer should be used. This should be stored in a well-

a   b

Figure 85 **a** and **b** Greasing a drive sprocket bearing.

Figure 86   Cleaning cylinder cooling fins.

labelled, leak-proof container approved for storing fuel.

Before refuelling, it is important to stop the engine, place the chainsaw in a clear area, and let it cool down. When refuelling a chainsaw, the chain-oil tank should also be refilled. Filler caps and areas of the body around them should be cleaned prior to undoing and refilling to minimise contamination.

Screws and nuts   Accessible screws and nuts should be tightened as required to prevent them shaking loose during chainsaw operation. *Never over-tighten nuts and screws* as stripped threads may result, particularly in components made of alloy or plastic.

Weekly maintenance

Maintenance procedures that should be carried out *weekly* include the following:

- grease the drive sprocket bearing;
- clean the cylinder cooling fins and cooling fan;
- check the starter rope for wear; and
- check the guide (cutter) bar for burrs and wear.

These tasks are described below.

Drive sprocket bearing   Greasing the drive sprocket bearing should be done sparingly using a high temperature grease. Some brands of chainsaw provide a grease hole in the end of the crankshaft which allows the bearing to be greased simply by using the same grease gun as that supplied for sprocket nosed guide bars. Other saws will require the removal of the clutch assembly and/or the clutch drum. As the procedure to remove the clutch will vary according to the make and model of saw, it is recommended that the owner's manual be consulted *before* attempting this task.

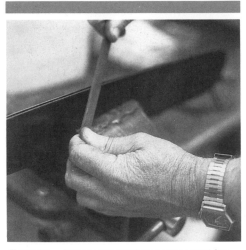

Figure 87   Removing the burr from a guide (cutter) bar.

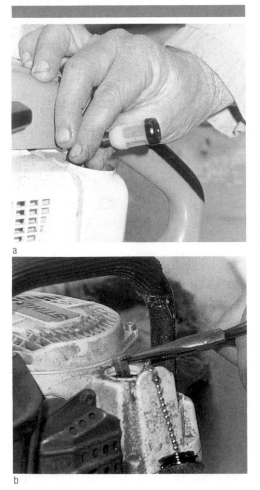

a

b

Figure 88   Removing fuel **a** and oil **b** filters for cleaning.

Cylinder cooling fins and the cooling fan These can be cleaned using an appropriate solvent and wooden scraper or compressed air. Access is usually gained by removing the fan/starter housing and cylinder cowling. Inside surfaces of housings and cowlings should also be cleaned thoroughly.

Starter rope If the starter rope is showing obvious wear, it should be replaced to eliminate the obvious problem of having it break on the job. The most common point of rope wear is within the first 200 mm where it first comes up against the engine compression.

Guide (cutter) bar Checking for wear and burrs should be carried out on the outside edges. If these are present, remove with a smooth flat file placed flat on the bar. File into the bar on all edges.

Uneven guide rails can sometimes be dressed square by using a flat file and a square. Alternatively, many chainsaw dealers have a guide bar dressing machine. After dressing the bar rails, check to ensure that correct bar groove depth is being maintained. There should be at least 1 mm clearance between the drive links and the bottom of the groove. It may be possible to have the bar re-grooved, but consideration should be given to discarding the bar and purchasing a new one.

Other problems such as bent bars, worn stellite tips or sprocket nose bearings, worn grooves, cracks and chips require specialist attention or replacement.

Other maintenance

It may sometimes be necessary to carry out maintenance operations other than those previously discussed — perhaps on a monthly basis. These may include:

- cleaning fuel and chain-oil filters;
- cleaning out the fuel and chain-oil tanks; and
- checking and servicing the spark plug.

Fuel and chain-oil filters These are fitted on the ends of flexible pick-up line found in each tank. To clean a filter, first remove the filler cap, then use a specially hooked or bent length of wire to 'fish out' the line and filter. The filter may then be removed from the pick-up line, washed in petrol and allowed to dry out before being refitted and replaced in the tank.

Fuel and chain-oil tanks The tanks may become contaminated despite care being taken to clean dirt and sawdust from around the filler caps before removing them. As condensation can also cause further contamination, it is necessary to flush these tanks out from time to time. This can be carried out using two-stroke fuel. At the same time it is a good idea to check that the vent hole in each filler cap is clean. Any obstructions can be cleared using compressed air.

Spark plug Maintenance of plugs is an integral part of chainsaw maintenance. Any chainsaw which is hard to start or tends to run unevenly should have its spark plug checked for cleanliness and correct gap. Where required, the spark plug can be cleaned and the gap reset with a good set of feeler gauges.

Chain and drive sprocket maintenance/ replacement

Most chain, guide (cutter) bar and sprocket problems and many chainsaw motor problems can be directly attributed to inadequate lubrication, incorrect chain tension or incorrect chain sharpening.

If the oil pump is working, the pick-up hole in the guide bar is clear (see 'Daily maintenance' above) and a good quality oil is used, then lubrication will not be a problem. There are specially formulated oils for bar and chain lubrica-

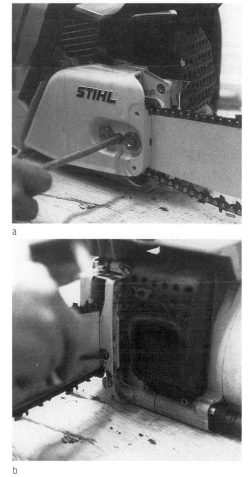

a

b

Figure 89 Chain tensioning.
a Tensioning screw accessed through sprocket cover.
b Tension screw located at side of guide bar.

tion that contain an additive to make them 'sticky' to resist being thrown off as the chain moves around the bar. *Always use a recommended chain and bar oil.* Never use waste oil, such as sump oil, for a chain and bar oil as such oils do not provide adequate lubrication and contain abrasive impurities that can damage oil pump mechanisms as well as causing undue wear to the bar and chain.

A simple method of checking that the chain is receiving adequate lubrication is to run the chainsaw with the nose of the guide bar a few centimetres above a suitable surface. If lubrication is adequate, a streak of oil should be seen.

Chain tensioning

To prevent cuts to the hands, strong work gloves should be worn when handling or tensioning saw chain.

Ideally, chain tensioning should be carried out before starting work, when the chain is cold, and then again after a break in operations such as a refuelling stop. It may sometimes be necessary to re-tension a sagging chain while work is still in progress — particularly on saws with long guide bars in hot weather. It is recommended that the chain be slackened off immediately cutting ceases, otherwise the cooling chain may shrink, causing damage — possibly even bending the crankshaft.

Cold tensioning begins by loosening the bar nuts sufficiently to allow the nose of the bar to move. The nose is then held up and tension applied to the chain by turning the chain tension screw located in the saw body or sprocket cover. A long conventional screwdriver is often better suited to this task than the combination tool supplied with the saw.

For solid nose bars the chain is correctly tensioned when the tie-straps touch the bottom guide (cutter) bar rails along their entire length. This tension should then be checked by *pulling* the chain around the bar several times and 'snapping' it clear of the bar rails after each rotation. At this point there should be *light* tension in the chain, but it should still pull freely around the bar. Sprocket nose bars require *more* chain tension than solid nose bars as insufficient tension will result in undue wear to the sprocket, bar and chain. A good test for both solid and sprocket nose bars is that the chain turns freely around the bar when pulled with two hands but, when pulled with one hand only, the whole chainsaw will slide across a smooth, flat surface such as a bench top, stump or log.

Finally, while still holding the nose of

the bar up, the bar and sprocket-cover retaining nuts should be tightened firmly.

Running in a new chain

Ideally, a new chain should be sharpened and soaked in oil overnight before use. This ensures that the chain is sharp and all moving parts are well lubricated prior to running in. Alternatively, the bar groove can be filled with oil and the chain liberally coated with oil. The chain is then fitted to the saw and tensioned correctly (see 'Chain tensioning'). The saw should then be started and the chain run at slow speed, not cutting wood, until it begins to sag. It should then be stopped, the chain re-tensioned, and extra oil applied to the bar and chain before running it at slow speed again for another one to two minutes. Stop the saw again and re-tension the chain. Proceed by making two or three light cuts, then check and re-tension the chain if necessary. Continue running in the chain with light work, stopping to re-tension as required.

Chain sharpening

Before attempting to sharpen a saw chain it is necessary to determine the type and size of chain as these will dictate the filing angles and the size of chainsaw file required. Only files manufactured specifically for sharpening saw chain are suitable.

Chain types available are chipper, semi-chisel, chisel and low profile. Chisel chains are ideal for falling as they enable fast cutting, but are easy to blunt. Chipper chains cut slowly, and were at one time the only 'modern' chains available. Arborists prefer semi-chisel chains since though not as fast as chisel chains, they do produce a smooth finished cut. These are illustrated. Different filing angles are used for each chain type, though there may be some variation between manufacturers. Cutter top plate filing angles vary from 30 degrees to 35 degrees, while side plate angles vary from 80 degrees to 90 degrees. Therefore, when purchasing a chain, one should enquire about the correct filing angles.

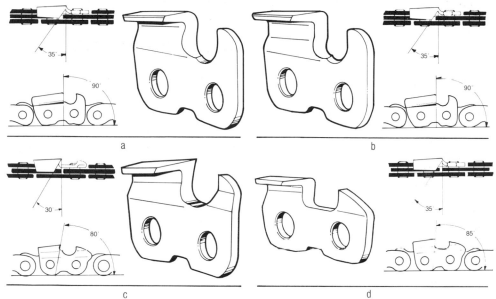

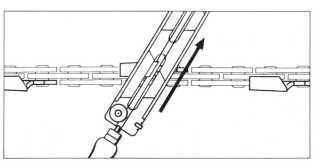

Figure 90 Chain types
a Chipper
b Semi-chisel
c Chisel (full chisel)
d Low profile (semi-chisel).

Figure 91 Filing chain cutters with a file and conventional guide.

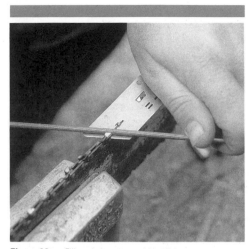

Figure 92   Filing chain cutters with a 'file-o-plate' guide.

Figure 93   Filing chain cutters with the aid of a roller guide.

Chain size can be determined by measuring the distance between any three rivets and dividing this measurement by two. The answer is referred to as the *chain pitch* and it is usually given in imperial measurements. Once the chain pitch has been determined, a chainsaw file of appropriate size can be selected for sharpening as per the table below.

Table 9   Chain pitches and file sizes

Chain pitch inches	File size required for sharpening (inches in diameter)
¼	5/32
.325	3/16
⅜	7/32
.404	7/32

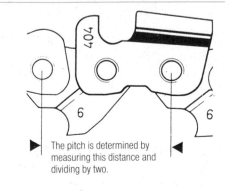

The pitch is determined by measuring this distance and dividing by two.

Figure 94   Chain pitch.

Before sharpening the chain, it is important to ensure that it is correctly tensioned and that the chainsaw is well secured. Various log vices can be useful for securing the bar when sharpening the chain 'on the job'.

When filing, only the correct size of chainsaw file should be used. However, where mcre than half the cutter has been filed away, it is advisable to use a chainsaw file of the next smaller size for sharpening. The possibility of filing the tie straps, leading to chain breakage, will then be lessened.

Each cutter should be filed from the inside to the outside. Since the file will only work when used in one direction (forward), do not apply pressure on the back (return) stroke and hold the file clear of the cutter. Each cutter should be filed to the same length; this can be achieved by filing each one with the same number of strokes.

Sharpening is required as soon as the cutters have lost their cutting edge. This may be necessary only once or many times per day depending on the type of wood being cut and the work conditions. Each cutter of a chain in this condition should only require two or three strokes of the file to restore its sharpness. If a chain is used after it has lost its cutting edge, or comes in contact with soil or a hard object such as a nail or

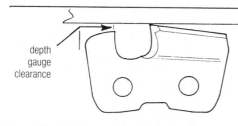

Figure 95   Depth gauge clearance.

rock, it may require more extensive sharpening.

As cutter top and side plates are chrome plated for abrasion resistance, it is important to check that this coating is not damaged. If the plating is damaged, it is necessary to file the cutter back to undamaged chrome as failure to do this will result in the cutter losing its edge quickly. Various guides can be used as aids in filing each cutter to the correct angles.

After sharpening, it is necessary to check the height of each depth gauge to ensure that the correct clearance is maintained. Where necessary a flat safety-edge file and depth gauge tool should be used to maintain this clearance by filing each depth gauge as illustrated. Following the use of conventional depth gauge tools, the front edge of each depth gauge should be rounded off with the flat file to maintain the original profile.

Any burrs can be removed from cutters by drawing a piece of wood (such as a chainsaw file handle) across them after sharpening.

Whenever the chain is removed from the guide bar, it should be examined for faults such as:

- broken rivets;
- broken or worn tie straps;
- damaged drive links; and
- broken or badly damaged cutters.

A chain with any of these faults should not be used as it may cause serious injury to the operator.

Eventually, it is no longer practical to re-sharpen a chain and it must be replaced. (Refer to 'Drive sprocket replacement' and 'Running in a new chain'.)

Figure 96   Maintaining depth gauge clearance with a conventional depth gauge tool.

Figure 97   Maintaining depth gauge clearance with a 'file-o-plate'.

Chain breaking and joining

From time-to-time it may be necessary to break and rejoin a saw chain.

Some reasons for this include:

Figure 98   Breaking a chain with a punch and purpose made backing plate.

- shortening a chain which has stretched beyond the capacity of the chain tensioning mechanism — this is more likely to occur on chainsaws with long guide bars;
- replacing damaged parts such as drive links and cutters; and
- making up new chain loops from bulk reels of chain.

A variety of tools is available to perform this task, both out on the job and in the workshop. Basically, all are used to punch out the old rivets and peen or spin new rivets to rejoin the tie straps as shown.

Drive sprocket replacement

The saw chain and drive sprocket should be considered as an integrated unit. Thus, when fitting a new chain, a new drive sprocket should also be fitted as the use of worn parts with new components causes premature wear of the new components.

Drive sprocket replacement intervals can be extended by alternating two chains of equal age with the one drive sprocket, and this can be done as part of daily maintenance. Also, the drive sprocket should be checked daily for wear. While spur sprockets are quite easy to check for

wear, rim sprockets require much closer inspection. Worn sprockets are illustrated.

a

b

Figure 99   Worn sprockets.
a Standard spur sprocket.
b Rim sprocket.

Carburettor tuning

To obtain optimum performance, maximise engine life and reduce operator stress, it may be necessary to adjust chainsaw carburettor settings from time-to-time. For example, a setting that is too 'rich' will result in loss of power and excessive exhaust, while a setting which is too 'lean' will also result in power loss and, ultimately, engine damage.

As the chainsaw carburettor is a complex component, when it is in need of repair it is better left to a competent chainsaw mechanic, however, the chainsaw operator should be able to carry out basic carburettor tuning. Before undertaking this operation, the following should be checked and rectified where necessary. Check if:

- the air filter is clean;
- the fuel filter is clean;
- the muffler/spark arrestor screen is clean;
- the spark plug is clean and correctly gapped; and
- the two-stroke fuel mix is of the correct petrol:oil ratio.

For all modern chainsaws it is recommended that a tachometer is used to accurately set engine speed to manufacturer's recommendations. To tune with a tachometer, simply set the high and low speed adjustment screws to the manufacturer's recommendation in the owner's manual. Then, with a chain and bar fitted, and using the tachometer, set the high speed screw to the manufacturer's recommended revolutions per minute (rpm).

Following these checks, the high and low speed adjustment screws should be set to the manufacturer's basic settings by *gently* turning in each screw until it *just* seats. Forcing the screws down into the seats will cause damage. Then turn each screw out to the manufacturer's recommended settings. The chainsaw should then be brought up to normal operating temperature by running it for a few minutes at fast idle.

To fine tune the carburettor when a tachometer is not available (after setting the high and low speed adjustment screws as described above), adjust the *low speed* mixture by slowly turning in the **low speed mixture screw** (leaning out the mixture) until the fastest smooth idle is attained. Now turn out the screw approximately one-quarter of a turn; at this setting the engine should not hesitate when the throttle is opened. The chain must not move when the engine is idling. If it is moving, it will be necessary to adjust the **idle speed adjustment screw**. This adjustment *does not affect mixture settings*.

To set the **high speed mixture screw**:

- run the engine at full throttle;
- slowly turn in the screw until the engine begins 'two stroking'*;
- immediately turn the screw out until

Figure 100 Using a tachometer to tune a chainsaw carburettor.

Figure 101 Carburettor adjustment screws.

the engine just begins 'four stroking'**; then
- turn the screw out another one-sixth to one-quarter of a turn.

At this setting, when the chainsaw is under load, the engine will cease 'four stroking', and will provide maximum performance. Note that the engine must be 'four stroking' when not under load.

---

* When 'two stroking' the engine will appear to be revving freely and firing evenly.
** When 'four stroking' the engine will appear to be missing or running unevenly.

If the engine is 'two stroking' when not under load, the mixture is too lean, lubrication is inadequate, and damage to the engine may result.

General chainsaw safety precautions

The chainsaw is a potentially dangerous tool, operation of which should only be carried out by fit, alert adults. Never operate a chainsaw or allow one to be operated by a person who is affected by drugs or alcohol. *Do not work alone* when using a chainsaw, just in case an accident occurs.

Some general safety precautions for using a chainsaw are listed below.

- Always *hold the chainsaw firmly with both hands* during use. Thumb and fingers should encircle the handles, the left hand on the front handle and right hand on the rear handle. The left arm should be rigid and the body positioned to the left of the chainsaw, so that, if 'kickback' should occur, the saw will come up the right-hand side of the body.
- *Ensure that the work area is clear of stones and other objects* that may cause the operator to lose balance. Stop the chainsaw and put it on the ground before moving cut branch material.
- *Do not cut above shoulder height.*
- Generally, *use only the straight sections of the guide bar* for cutting in order to prevent contact with the upper quadrant of the bar nose, causing 'kickback'.
- When using a chainsaw, *keep it close to the body* and keep a secure footing and well balanced stance in order to maintain control.
- Run the chainsaw *in only well ventilated areas*. Keep exhaust gases directed away from you.
- *Wear protective clothing* such as the following, when using a chainsaw:
  safety helmet
  visor/safety glasses
  ear muffs
  gloves
  trousers/chaps made of kevlar chain-guard fabric
  non-snag clothing
  non-skid steel toe-capped work boots
  high visibility clothing as required in public areas.
- A *first aid kit* which includes large and small wound dressings, should be readily accessible at all times.
- *Ensure that people and animals are outside the immediate work area.*

Appendices

Appendix 1:
Sailmaker's whipping

Sailmaker's whipping is recommended for seizing the ends of ropes such as nylon lifelines and lowering ropes. Manilla or linen twine of about 1 mm diameter is used for this purpose. The twine should be waxed by running it over a block of beeswax before making the sailmaker's whip, as this should make it easier to work with and less subject to rotting.

In the case of nylon ropes that have been whipped, the ends may also be heated to melt the nylon fibres together, thus sealing the ends.

Figure 102   **a–p** Sailmakers whipping.

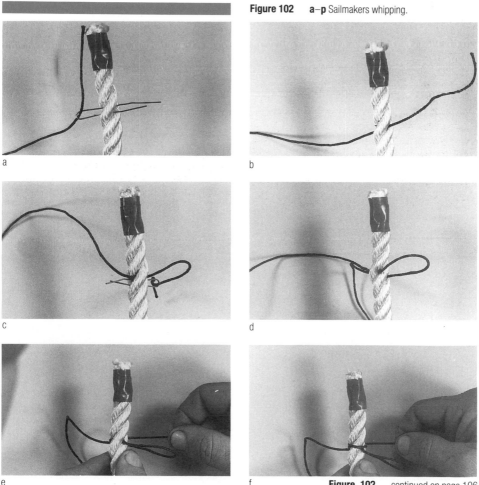

a

b

c

d

e

f   **Figure 102**   continued on page 106

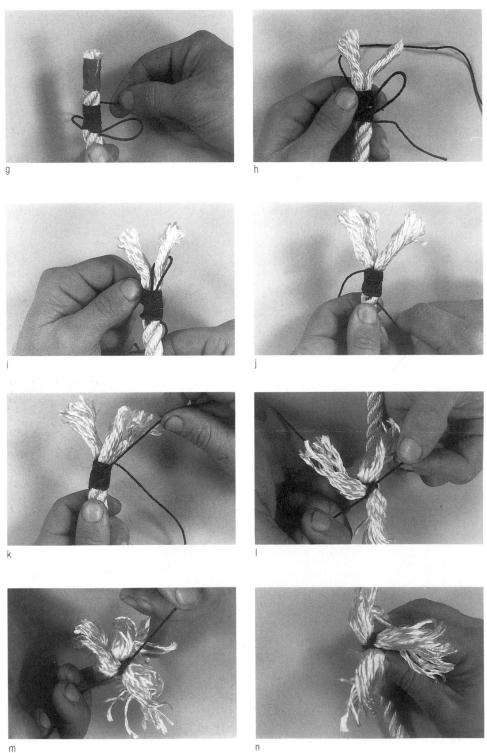

g

h

i

j

k

l

m

n

Figure 102   *(continued)*

o

p

Appendix 2:
Eye-splicing

Eye-splicing is a method of forming a permanent loop or 'eye' at the end of a rope. Tool strops are often made of rope, generally manilla, by this means. The installation of thimbles in ropes, such as winch ropes, can protect the eye-splice from wear.

Ends of individual rope strands should be seized by tying or taping to prevent them from undoing while making the eye-splice.

Figure 103 **a–j** Eye splicing.

a

b

c

d

Figure 103 continued on page 108

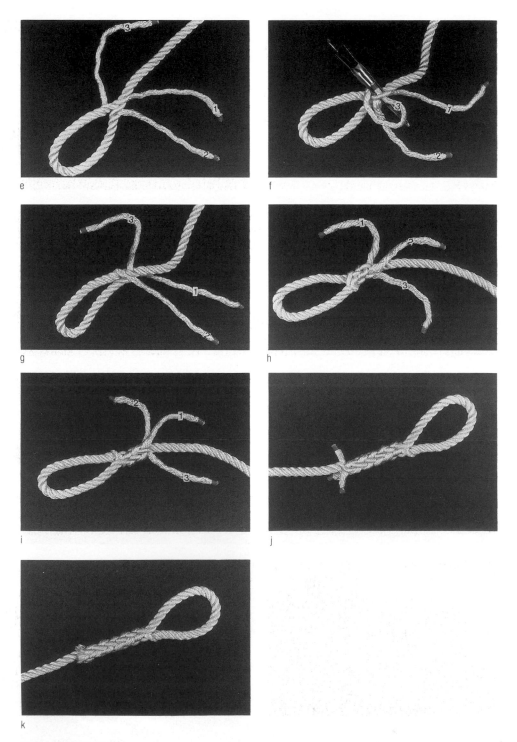

e

f

g

h

i

j

k

Figure 103   *(continued)*

Appendix 3:
Bowline on the bight

The bowline on the bight can be used for joining additional winch rope to a winch cable that is too short. The knot is ideal for this purpose since it is easy to untie after having a heavy load placed on it.

Figure 104   **a–h** Bowline on a bight.

a

b

c

d

e

f

g

Figure 104   continued on page 110

h

Figure 104 *(continued)*

Appendix 4:
Electronic detection of decay in trees

For many years research workers have experimented with the use of electrical current in an attempt to distinguish between dead and living plant tissues, and to detect decay in wood.

As a result of this work, the first instrument utilising current, the Shigometer, became commercially available in the United States for use by arborists. Developed in the early 1970s, this tool measures resistance of the vascular tissues to direct pulsed current. Later, in the late 1970s and early 1980s another instrument, the Plant Impedance Ratio Meter (PIRM), was developed in Australia. This machine utilises alternating currents at two different frequencies, 1 kHz and 10 kHz. Admittance values are recorded and, as admittance is the reverse of impedance, the impedance ratios are calculated by dividing high frequency by low frequency admittances.

The electrical admittance and electrical resistance of healthy plant tissues varies with both the depth of tissue probed and the water status of stems. However, impedance ratios remain relatively constant for healthy tissue and changes are independent of probing depth. Changes in impedance ratios recorded for healthy bark tissues are constantly higher than those from tissues which have been damaged by pathogenic activity.

Electrical resistance and impedance will also vary seasonally and may have quite low readings during periods of high cambial activity. Variations in temperature may also affect readings.

Both the Shigometer and the PIRM have two types of probes: a short twin needle probe for testing the phloem and cambial tissues and a longer twisted wire probe for testing decay in xylem tissues. These long probes require a small diameter hole (or series of holes) to be drilled into the plant, creating a small wound.

To enable accurate interpretation of readings, a database should be established by testing many trees of a species within a locality, taking into account the variable factors mentioned above.

Before either instrument can become an everyday tool for the use of all arborists, there is still a great deal of research work and data collection to be carried out.

Glossary of terms

abscission natural shedding of plant parts, such as leaves and fruit.

apical dominance the control exerted by the terminal bud (or bud cluster) over the lateral buds of a currently elongating shoot.

arborial mammal, a tree-dwelling animal that suckles its young, for example, possums and squirrels.

bacteria simple microscopic unicellular organisms.

bark cambium (phellogen) thin layer of actively dividing cells responsible for the formation of cork or outer bark.

bast phloem or inner bark.

bight 1 an open loop of rope;
  2 any slack part of rope between two ends.

branch-bark ridge zone of raised bark found in the upper side of the branch/trunk union.

branch collar branch tissue development early in the growing season, forming a collar of branch tissue at the base of a branch.

bud immature flower and/or shoot with meristematic tissue enclosed in protective scale leaves.

butt base of trunk or branch.

callus 1 undifferentiated, non-lignified cell growth derived from the cambium in response to wounding;
  2 differentiated, lignified cells produced at wound margins (more correctly known as 'wound wood').

cambium thin layer of actively dividing cells responsible for the formation of vascular tissue.

compartmentalisation process by which decay is resisted by the tree.

crotch junction of two or more branches.

crown region of tree from which main limbs originate.

cultivar an 'improved' species produced by breeding in cultivation.

disease unhealthy condition.

epicormic growth developing from a dormant or latent bud.

fastigiate tapering or conical growth habit.

fungus simple form of plant life devoid of chlorophyll, that lives on organic matter.

guying securing newly planted advanced trees with cables.

heartwood old xylem cells which, although no longer conductive, provide support and can respond to injury or pathogens. In some trees extractives may be deposited in these cells causing them to be a different colour to the active cells.

heeled in temporarily planted.

111

insects small invertebrate segmented animal typically having three main body sections (head, thorax and abdomen), four wings, and three pairs of five-jointed legs.

instar stage of development of an insect or mite with an incomplete life cycle.

kerf saw cut.

kickback a dangerous, forceful, upward and rearward movement of the chainsaw cutter bar, usually in the direction of the operator.

larva grub, maggot or caterpillar stage of insect development.

lateral an annual growth of appreciable length.

macro-organisms organisms such as beetles, millipedes, worms etc. that are visible without magnification.

main leader lateral which terminates a main limb.

main limb a main branch in a tree's framework.

meristem actively dividing plant cells capable of developing into specialised plant tissue and organs.

metamorphosis development of an insect or mite through distinct stages.

micro-organisms organisms such as some fungi, bacteria, etc. that are only visible with magnification.

mite minute invertebrate animal, typically having eight legs.

mutation variation in an organism due to genetic change.

mycelium mass of fungal threads (hyphae) comprising the body of a fungus.

node the part of a stem at which a leaf and/or bud arises.

nymph immature stage of development resembling the adult.

parasite organism dependent on another living organism.

pathogen agent that causes disease.

pH measure of acidity or alkalinity.

phellogen see bark cambium.

pheromone a substance secreted by an insect.

phloem the conductive cells on the inner side of the bark cambium which primarily transport photosynthates from the leaves to all other parts of the plant.

pupa resting stage in the development of an insect.

reeve to pass a rope through a thimble or sheeve.

rootstock stock on which the tree has been budded or grafted.

saprophyte organism depending on non-living organic matter.

sapwood actively conducting xylem elements.

scaffold limbs main limbs.

secondary limbs limbs arising from main limbs.

snig to drag a log or tree, usually behind a vehicle.

spores minute reproductive cells.

sucker a growth arising from the rootstock or base of a tree.

swarf sawdust produced as the result of boring.

tracheid an elongated, lignified element of the xylem responsible for conduction and strength.

trunk collar trunk tissue development late in the growing season that encircles a branch collar, thereby forming a collar of trunk tissues around the base of a branch.

variety naturally occurring variant within a species.

vigour volume of annual growth.

wound wood see 'callus'.

xylem vascular tissue that conducts water and minerals.

References and further reading

Arboriculture/tree surgery/pruning/tree care

Anon. (1966). *British Standard 3998: 1966, Recommendations for Tree Work*. British Standards Institution, UK.

Anon. (1985). *Caring for Trees*. State Electricity Commission of Victoria, Melbourne.

Bridgeman, P.H., Jordan, P.J. and Patch, D. (1976). *Tree Surgery: A Complete Guide*. David and Charles, UK.

Brown, G.E. (1972). *The Pruning of Trees, Shrubs and Conifers*. Faber, UK.

Grigor, J. (1868). *Arboriculture*. Edmanston and Douglas, Scotland.

Hadlington, P.W. and Johnston, J.A. (1988). *Australian Trees: A Guide to Their Care and Repair*. NSW University Press, Sydney.

Harris, R.W. (1983). *Arboriculture: Care of Trees, Shrubs and Vines in the Landscape*. Prentice-Hall, USA.

Hawker, J., Price, B., Simpfendorfer, K. and Ashton, J. (1984). *A Guide for the Management and Care of Trees*. The Register of Significant Trees Committee of the National Trust of Australia (Victoria) and the Royal Botanic Gardens, Melbourne.

Kilpatrick, D.T. (1968). *Pruning for the Australian Gardener*. Rigby, Adelaide.

Pirone, P.P. (1972). *Tree Maintenance*. Oxford University Press, USA.

Richardson, M. (1985). *The Care and Maintenance of Trees, Management Aid No. 7*. Royal Australian Institute of Parks and Recreation, Canberra.

Shigo, A.L. and Marx, H.G. (1974). *Your Tree's Trouble May Be You*. Forest Service, United States Department of Agriculture, Agriculture Information Bulletin No. 372.

Shigo, A.L. and Marx, H.G. (1976). *Rx for Wounded Trees*. Forest Service, United States Department of Agriculture, Agriculture Information Bulletin No. 387.

Shigo, A.L. and Marx, H.G. (1977). *Compartmentalization of Decay in Trees*. Forest Service, United States Department of Agriculture, Agriculture Information Bulletin No. 405.

Shigo, A.L. (1979). *Tree Decay: An Expanded Concept*. Forest Service, United States Department of Agriculture, Agriculture Information Bulletin No. 419.

Shigo, A.L. (1986). *A New Tree Biology*. Shigo and Trees, Associates, USA.

Shigo, A.L. (1986). *A New Tree Biology Dictionary*. Shigo and Trees, Associates, USA.

Shigo, A.L. (1989). *Tree Pruning: A Worldwide Photo Guide*. Shigo and Trees, Associates, USA.

Tree falling, trimming and crosscutting

National Forest Industries Training Council Ltd, *Work Technique for Chainsaw Users*, Victoria, 1991.

Amenity tree valuation

Anon. (1973). *Draft Australian Standard Method of Tree Evaluation (Metric Units)*. DR 73030. Standards Association of Australia.

Anon. (1975). *Formula To Be Used for Assessing the Economic Value of Ornamental Trees in Public Open Spaces Under the Control of the Parks, Gardens and Recreations Committee of the Melbourne City Council*. Melbourne City Council, Victoria.

Anon. (1976). *An Evaluation Method for Amenity Trees*. The Tree Council, UK.

Australian Institute of Horticulture Inc. (1977). *A Method for Assessing the Monetary Value of Trees Used in Amenity Horticulture, Technical Memorandum No. 1*. Victorian State Council, Australian Institute of Horticulture.

Wycherley, P.R. (1976). Towards a national method of valuing amenity trees. *Australian Parks and Recreation* May: 41–43. Royal Institute of Parks and Recreation, Canberra.

Wycherley, P.R. (1979). *Amenity tree valuation — a working paper*. Supplement to *Australian Parks and Recreation*. Royal Australian Institute of Parks and Recreation, Canberra.

Selection of trees

Anon. (no date). *Design and Siting Guidelines: Bushfire Protection for Rural Houses*. Country Fire Authority, Victoria.

Anon. (1985). *Guide to Tree Planting near Powerlines: A Description of Suitable Varieties*. State Electricity Commission of Victoria, Melbourne.

Anon. (annual). *Planter's Handbook and Tree List and Trees for Farm and Roadside Planting*. Natural Resources Conservation League of Victoria, Melbourne.

Anon. (leaflets). *Planting near Drains and Sewers*.
Trees for Special Purposes.
Trees for the Northern Slopes of Victoria.
Trees for the Western Plains of Victoria.
Department of Conservation Forests and Lands of Victoria, Melbourne.

Anon. (leaflets). *Seaside Tree and Shrub Plantings for Coastal New South Wales*.
Tree Roots and Building Structures.
Trees for Heavy or Clay Soils.
Trees for Planting in New England.
Trees for Planting in the Southern and Central Tablelands of New South Wales.
Trees for Planting in Southern Coastal New South Wales.
Trees for Planting in the Western Plains Region of New South Wales.
Trees for the South West Riverina and Murrumbidgee Irrigation Area.
Trees for the Western Slopes of New South Wales (including Upper Hunter Valley).

Trees for Soils on Hawkesbury Sandstone.
Forestry Commission of New South Wales.
Anon. *Western Suburbs Tree and Shrub Planting Guide.* (leaflet). Royal Botanic Gardens, Melbourne.
Anon. *500 Australian Native Plants.* Society for Growing Australian Plants, Maroondah Group, Victoria.
Anon. *Planting near Overhead Powerlines.* (leaflet). Electricity Trust of South Australia.
Arthur, T. and Martin, D. (1981). *Street Tree Directory.* Royal Australian Institute of Parks and Recreation, Victoria.
Australian Plant Study Group. (1983). *Grow What Where?* Nelson, Melbourne.
Brown, A. and Hall, N. (1968). *Growing Trees on Australian Farms.* Forestry and Timber Bureau, Canberra.
Costermans, L.F. (1981). *Native Trees and Shrubs of South-eastern Australia.* Rigby, Adelaide.
Hall, N. (Ed.) (1972). *The Use of Trees and Shrubs in the Dry Country of Australia.* Forestry and Timber Bureau, Canberra.
Lord, E.E. and Willis, J.H. (1982). *Shrubs and Trees for Australian Gardens.* Lothian, Melbourne.
Pike, J. (1981). *Trees for Southern Victoria: A Guide to Identification and Use.* Landarc, Victoria.
Rowell, R.J. (1980). *Ornamental Flowering Trees Australia.* Reed, Sydney.
Simpfendorfer, K.J. (1975). *An Introduction to Trees for South-eastern Australia.* Inkata Press, Melbourne.

Pests, diseases, weeds and their control

Beardsell, D.V. *What To Do if Trees are Suspected of Being Affected by Natural Gas in the Soil: A Recommended Procedure.* Standing Committee comprising the Department of Agriculture, Melbourne City Council, Municipal Association, and the Gas and Fuel Corporation of Victoria.
Carne, P.B., Crawford, L.D., Fletcher, M.J., Galloway, I.D. and Highley, E. (1980). *Scientific Names of Insects and Allied Forms Occurring in Australia.* CSIRO, Melbourne.
Ferro, D.N. (1978). *New Zealand Insect Pests.* Lincoln University College of Agriculture, New Zealand.
French, J.D.R. (1981). Urban forests for improving air quality. *Arboriculture Australia* (1).
Hadlington, P.W. and Johnston, J.A. (1982). *An Introduction to Australian Insects.* NSW University Press, Sydney.
Hadlington, P.W. and Gerozsis, J. (1985). *Urban Pest Control in Australia.* NSW University Press, Sydney.
Hassall, KA. (1982). *The Chemistry of Pesticides, Their Metabolism, Mode of Action and Uses in Crop Protection.* Macmillan, UK.
Hely, P.C., Pasfield, G. and Gellatley, J.G. (1982). *Insect Pests of Fruit and Vegetables in NSW.* Inkata Press, Melbourne.
Hyde-Wyatt, B.H. and Morris, D.I. (1975). *Tasmanian Weed Handbook.* Tasmanian Department of Agriculture, Hobart.
Hyde-Wyatt, B.H. and Morris, D.I. (1980). *The Noxious and Secondary Weeds of Tasmania.* Tasmanian Department of Agriculture, Hobart.

Jones, D.L. and Elliot, W.R. (1986). *Pests, Diseases and Ailments of Australian Plants*. Lothian, Melbourne.

Kerruish, R.M. and Unger, P.W. (1989). *Plant Protection Parts 1 and 2*. Rootrot Press, Canberra.

Marks, G.C., Fuhrer, B.A., Walters, N.E.M. and Huebner, M.L. (Eds) (1982). *Tree Diseases of Victoria*. Forests Commission, Victoria.

McMaugh, J. (1985). *What Garden Pest Is That?* Lansdowne, Sydney.

Pirone, P.P. (1978). *Diseases and Pests of Ornamental Plants*. Wiley, USA.

Tattar, T.A. (1978). *Diseases of Shade Trees*. Academic Press, USA.

Vock, N.T. (1978). *A Handbook of Plant Diseases in Colour: Vol. 1, Fruit and Vegetables*. Queensland Department of Primary Industries, Brisbane.

Wheeler, B.E.J. (1969). *An Introduction to Plant Diseases*. Wiley, UK.

Worthing, C.A. (Ed.) (1983). *The Pesticide Manual*. The British Crop Protection Council, UK.

Materials/equipment

Anon. (1985, 1986). *Manual of Uniform Traffic Control Devices*. Australian Standards Association.

Anon. (no date). *Waratah Wire Rope, General Information*. Australian Wire Industries Pty Ltd.

Anon. (leaflets). *Instructions for Operators of Elevating Platform Vehicles*.
   Tree Felling and Trimming: Instructions for the Guidance and Safety of Employees. State Electricity Commission, Victoria.

Hall, W. (1977). *Barnarcle Parp's Chainsaw Guide*. Rodale, USA.

Harvesting Research Group, Division of Forest Research, CSIRO. *Work Technique in Pine Thinning*. CSIRO, Canberra.

National Forest Industries Training Council. *Work Technique for Chainsaw Users*. Victoria, 1991.

Botany/plant physiology

Abercrombie, M., Hickman, C.J. and Johnson, M.L. (1974). *Dictionary of Biology*. Penguin, UK.

Debenham, C. *The Language of Botany*. Society for Growing Australian Plants.

Dittmer, H.J. (1972). *Modern Plant Biology*. Van Nostrand, USA.

Edlin, H., Nimmo, M., et al. (1978). *The Illustrated Encyclopaedia of Trees, Timbers and Forests of the World*. Salamander, UK.

Morgan, D. (Ed.) (1972). *Biological Science: The Web of Life*. Australian Academy of Science, Canberra.

Stearn, W.T. (1983). *Botanical Latin*. David and Charles, UK.

Tippett, J.T. and Barclay, J.L. (1987). Detection of bark lesions caused by *Phytophthora cinnamomi* in *Eucalyptus marginata* with the Plant Impedance Ratio Meter and the Shigometer. *Canadian Journal of Forest Research* 17: 1228–1233.

Usher, G. (1966). *A Dictionary of Botany*. Constable, UK.

Weier, T.E., Barbour, M.G., Stocking, C.R. and Rost, T.L. (1982). *Botany, an Introduction to Plant Biology*. Wiley, USA.

Yeates, J.S. and Campbell, E.O. (1968). *Agricultural Botany*. Technical Correspondence School, New Zealand Department of Education.

Plant identification (general)

Bailey, L.H. (1976). *Hortus Third: A Concise Dictionary of Plants Cultivated in the United States and Canada*. Macmillan, USA.

Beckett, K.A. (1983). *The Concise Encyclopaedia of Garden Plants*. Orbis, UK.

Huxley, A., Griffiths, M. and Levy, M. (Eds) (1992). *The New Royal Horticultural Society Dictionary of Gardening*, 4 vols.

Index